Who Is Casey Anthony?

Who Is Casey Anthony?
Understanding the Motherly Motivation to Murder

Dr. Leslie Seppinni

Foreword by Mark Geragos

Published in Nashville, Tennessee by Dunham Books. For information regarding special sales or licensing, please contact the publisher:

Dunham Books
63 Music Square East
Nashville, Tennessee 37203
www.dunhamgroupinc.com

Trade Paperback ISBN: 978-0-9839-9062-8
Ebook ISBN: 978-0-9839-9063-5

Printed in the United States of America

Dedication

To Little Mr. Sunshine
May the twinkle in your eyes and bright smile forever
shine upon us;
may your laughter forever remind us to never take
ourselves too seriously;
and may your enthusiasm, adventures and passion keep us
interested and interesting.

—Love Always and Eternally

Table of Contents

Foreword by Mark Geragos   ix

Introduction   1

Chapter One: The Facts of the Case   7

Chapter Two: The American Phenomenon: Mothers Who Kill   31

Chapter Three: No Room for Excuses   47

Chapter Four: Emotional DNA   65

Chapter Five: Red Flags, Telltale Signs, and Hindsights   89

Chapter Six: The Verdict Is In   115

Endnotes   127

Acknowledgements   137

About the Author   139

Foreword
Mark Geragos

In nearly three decades, I have tried many cases, many of them highly publicized. But it's rare that a case captures the public imagination like the Casey Anthony trial. There are a multitude of reasons for this, but foremost was the involvement of her parents as the family saga unfolded. As a result of the parental entanglement in Casey Anthony's behavior, the public became fascinated with her background and the formation of her psychological makeup. After her family, friends, and previous co-workers gave numerous statements and interviews, intimately testifying under oath, the public came to the conclusion that this young mother, Casey, could go on a one-month party binge as her little girl, Caylee, rotted in a swamp.

Dr. Leslie Seppinni has carefully analyzed the statements, interviews, and testimony of Casey Anthony's parents, family, and friends, and assiduously researched women that have murdered their children to write the authoritative psychological assessment of Casey Anthony. Dr. Seppinni provides the raw facts, information, and the psychological profile of women who kill in cold blood to allow each reader to come to their own conclusion of who is Casey Anthony?

Unlike other books and experts surrounding the Casey Anthony story and trial, Dr. Seppinni focused on the fascination of Casey

Anthony beyond the public's outcry of justice for Caylee. Casey's sociological significance is symbolic of the reality of human nature. Dr. Seppinni's thesis is that mothers are "human beings first, women second and mothers third," and, if perceived in that order, they are just as capable of good and evil as men.

In this book, Dr. Seppinni identifies what she feels are stereotypical views of women. She then sets out to dissuade the reader of those stereotypes. Dr. Seppinni argues that because of harsh economic times, women are moving at a faster rate than anticipated into white-collar jobs, replacing men. Men now share a larger percentage of what still is considered traditional "women's work," and parental involvement as stay at home dads. Accordingly, the outcome of the differential power dynamic is shifting dramatically. Women no longer feel silence; for the first time they are speaking out about the reality of raising children and areas of dissatisfaction. Thus, we will continue to see more and more characteristics often defined as "male" obliterating traditional stereotypes.

Casey Anthony became a proxy for the MTV pop-culture, reality generation whose relevance, as Dr. Seppinni characterizes it, revolves around sex, drama, and risk taking behaviors. Seemingly an obvious observation, however, her surprising look leads us to focus on our future generations. She predicts that as generations progress, the traditional lines and roles of men and women will continue to shift and blend. As incarceration rates for women rise for increasingly violent crimes, Dr. Seppinni's underlying idea is essential of how this shift causes understandable vulnerability and societal concern. Casey Anthony is exememplary of the relevance of our young women and men, and the consequences that can ensue. Her thesis is that these characteristics were there all along, but because of society's need to believe women, and particularly mothers, are our saviors. This shift is discomforting. She argues that our ideal of mothers as the nurturers and supplying an endless bound of unconditional love "if our mother does not love us then who will."

Dr. Seppinni draws our attention to the outcome of a haunting lack of emotional security, loneliness in our lives, a black hole in our heart and soul, and fear of going out in the world with conviction that we can succeed. She concedes that our need to maintain our view of mothers as sacred damages our ability to develop coping strategies and an emotional safety net with all that is evil, wrong, and macabre.

Dr. Seppinni's book argues that we must gain a more balanced view of women in order to permit justice, protection of our children, and human rights. Women who have the emotional capability to murder their children is not new, nor is it always excusable by mental illness. Dr. Seppinni's book reminds the reader that society must come to accept that women, like men, have the same lust for power/dominance, love, money, lifestyle, and, in some cases, revenge.

The fascination with Casey Anthony finds its genesis in the lack of acceptance that a single white, sexy, middle-class woman living in the south could commit a murder of her own child in cold blood. Then the media sounded a drumbeat for her conviction as if she was already walking to her death. This further played upon the public's demand for justice for Caylee. The nation's total disbelief and anger at the jury's verdict of "Not Guilty" led to death threats to the jury, and a single-minded public conviction that Casey must pay and will pay. In an ironic twist to the most recent trial of the century, this book explores the inequities involving the punishment of men versus women. That take away is worth the read alone and yet there is so much more.

As a final point, Dr. Seppinni's tragedy to triumph life story combined with her years as a Crisis Intervention Specialist working out in the field and with corporate managers and high level executives who were suicidal, homicidal, or both, lends more than just a psychological assessment. This book provides answers to burning questions raised at trial. The most provocative and interesting look into the fascination and mind of *Who Is Casey Anthony?*

If you read only one book on the historic trial and conviction of Casey Anthony, then this is it!

Introduction

The first thing people think of, of course, is a couch. Leather preferably. And just long enough to stretch your legs out and close your eyes before a spectacled-individual with a clipboard sits upright in a chair, saying exactly what you've been wanting to hear your entire life: *And how does that make you feel?* And then this spectacled-individual nods, jotting notes with a pencil, while saying, "I understand. Continue please."

Psychologists, albeit like people in most professions, get painted into a stereotype. We are people who talk about "feelings." We're overly analytical and manipulative, enabling and opinionated. But psychology is much more than being a willing listener; it's the science of personality and behavioral understanding. Our clinical presentation and perception of an individual is not rooted in personal opinion or preference, but on diagnostic criteria that is backed by training, real life experience, research, and strict, concrete guidelines. Psychology is getting to the root of why people do what they do—a critical discovery when it comes to the criminal world and with cases like the now infamous *The State of Florida v. Casey Marie Anthony*.

From the beginning, like most people, I was glued to the case. Everyone was fascinated and horror-struck by the possibility that a mother could have potentially murdered her own daughter, a precious two year old, in cold blood. Home videos taken by the Anthony family showed Americans that Caylee was a beautiful, vibrant, and healthy little girl. It seemed like she was well loved by her mother and by her grandparents. But something wasn't quite right. If this was the case—if she was loved, prized, and treasured—what was her mother, Casey, doing?

Most of us would expect that when a mother finds out her child has been killed, or potentially murdered, that she would be devastated. Heartbroken. Almost unable to cope. She would want answers and justice. But the Casey we began to see in the media didn't match up with the Casey we saw in the videos. There was no guilt, no grief, no emotion. If anything, it was the opposite. She lied continually, intentionally misleading police, partied at night, and didn't report her daughter missing for thirty-one days. She acted like she was on Spring Break, not living her worst nightmare.

Immediately, there was a backlash. The public hadn't been so involved or outraged about a trial since a white Bronco charged down the Interstate. How could a mother who just lost her daughter be so indifferent? So manipulative? So uncaring? Quickly, Casey infamously earned the name "Tot Mom" by her number one antagonist, Nancy Grace. Society rallied against her. Casey was arguably the most hated woman in America.

As a doctor of clinical psychology, as well as a licensed marriage and family therapist with specialty in crisis intervention, I watched the case closely. And not just the talking heads or the newspaper scraps, but all the evidence, the reactions, and the body language. I also paid close attention to the reaction of the public. The outrage was palpable. Something was going on here beyond the traditional mold. Why were people so outraged at this particular murder? Why was everyone so fascinated with Casey? Sad though it is to say, people are murdered every day and often we can go on with our lives, relatively unfettered. But this case was different. It unnerved us. But why?

Casey Anthony angered the populous because she tampered with our perception of motherly love. Her irresponsibility and selfishness, which we barely scratched the surface of at the trial, showed us a side to women and mothers that we don't want to admit is there. As a whole, society has difficulty coming to terms with women behaving in male-defined aggressive patterns. Mothers are universally considered to be the nurturing gatekeepers of the home. The "sacred Madonas." As a result, we strongly resist believing that women can kill their children because, if this is true, the world is tilted. Anything is possible. Mothers are supposed to provide, protect, and give endlessly. So what do we do when the opposite occurs? How do we respond when a mother takes her child's life?

I began to realize that the public ultimately wanted to have greater insight, access, and knowledge about who Casey Anthony is, as well as a more thorough understanding of how prevalent her alleged actions are in society. Was this a one-time case, limited only to Tot Mom? Or are her alleged actions more widespread? Are the mothers who surround us in daily life—our neighbors, co-workers, and family members—capable of equal atrocity? If so, do they have specific characteristics or symptoms? Do they have to be mentally ill, or do women in their right mind follow through with the greatest sin?

As you read this book, I hope you begin to understand that discovering truth is about *not* being married to perceptions. Limiting someone to a stereotype only limits reality.

While my psychology background certainly helps me see this case from a unique angle, my personal experiences have further engrained in me that the human capacity for all things is infinite: both good and evil, kindness and abuse, fortitude and weakness.

I was born to a white mother and a black father. When I was young, my dad was sent to Sing-Sing for murder. I remember visiting him in the prison, having jailhouse conversations. My mother was still around at the time. She was physically beautiful, classy and elegant; to the world she was entirely charming and charismatic. But, inevitably, the State of New York declared her an unfit mother and I spent my early childhood years in foster care. At the age of fifteen, I was a victim of sexual assault.

Expectations followed me around my entire life. People expected me to turn out a certain way because of what I endured and where I came from. I was a mix-race, foster child, bred in poverty. But, thankfully, I grew up believing deeply in excuse free living. Just because I might be more prone to act a certain way or because it might be more understandable if I did, never has meant and never will mean that I have the excuse to behave in a certain way. Our backgrounds and experiences are not crutches unless we let them be.

The crux of the Casey Anthony case is rooted in both of these concepts: societal perception and excuse. On one side, society expects Casey to behave as all mothers are expected to behave. She is supposed to cherish her daughter, love her, and do everything for her. We expect this even more so as she is a young, attractive, white woman from a good middle class family. But Casey didn't fit the mother mold and, as a result, people grew outraged. They demanded answers. Why did she act the way she did? What *excuse* could possibly be good enough?

My goal in writing *Who Is Casey Anthony* is manifold. I want to discuss, in depth, the power of societal stereotypes, as well as our culture's need and ability to excuse away the truth. Moreover, it's important for us to understand how our reliance on excuse-inclined living is detrimental to our society's growth and wellbeing.

Additionally, I want to provide everyone with accessible, easy-to-understand information about filicide, offering expert psychological insight into who kills, why they kill, and how. While we will focus specifically on Casey, her motivations, and her alleged crimes, we'll also look at the much bigger picture. Casey is a template for understanding a much larger, highly complex issue that has a tremendous impact on society and the nuclear family. And for the sake of both of those, we will dig deep and be vitally honest about the motherly motivation to murder. In taking off our rosy glasses and being willing to see the world for how it is—learning to accept and identify why women kill and how—we can honor Caylee and prevent similar future and unnecessary tragedies from occurring.

Chapter One
The Facts of the Case

"How in the world can a mother wait thirty days before ever reporting her child missing? That's insane. That's bizarre. Something's just not right about that. Well, the answer is actually relatively simple. She never was missing. Caylee Anthony died on June 16, 2008, when she drowned in her family's swimming pool. As soon as Casey came around this corner and went back, she saw George Anthony holding Caylee in his arms. She immediately grabbed Caylee and began to cry. And cry. And cry. And shortly thereafter, George began to yell at her, 'Look what you've done. Your mother will never forgive you, and you will go to jail for child neglect for the rest of your frickin' life.'"[1]

Referring to the Anthonys as "a family of lies and secrets," defense attorney Jose Baez boldly addressed the jury in his opening arguments. His accusation was stunning, but it certainly wasn't the only audacious claim that would be made that day. The trial of *The State of Florida v. Casey Marie Anthony* was a circus of lies and deceit, but sadly for Caylee and those who sought true justice, not nearly enough hard evidence.

The opening statements began in Orlando, virtually three years after Caylee Anthony, a two year old girl, was reported missing and then found dead in December 2008. Her mother, Casey Anthony, only twenty-two years old at the time of Caylee's death, was charged with first degree murder, aggravated manslaughter of a child, aggravated child abuse, and providing false information to law enforcement. If convicted, she faced the death penalty.

The prosecution claimed Casey murdered her daughter by administering chloroform, then applying duct tape to her mouth. They argued that Casey, keen on an independent, partying lifestyle, sought freedom from her responsibilities, and, in turn, her daughter.

"When you have a child, that child becomes your life," argued Jeff Ashton, for the prosecution. "This case is about the clash between that responsibility, and the expectations that go with it, and the life that Casey Anthony wanted to have."[2]

On the other side, Baez, the defense attorney, claimed Casey's father, George Anthony, found the body in the family pool and that he helped dispose of Caylee's body. Baez even went so far as to suggest that George planted evidence to implicate his daughter and avert suspicion from himself. But undoubtedly Baez's most powerful move was that he keyed in on the power of human empathy.

"What makes this case unique is the family that it happened to," Baez said. "You will hear stories about a family that is incredibly dysfunctional, you will hear about ugly things, secret things, things that people don't speak about... On June 16, 2008, after Caylee died, Casey did what she's been doing all her life, hiding her pain, going into that dark corner and pretending that she does not live in the situation that she's living in. . . it all began when Casey was eight years old and her father came into her room and began to touch her inappropriately and it escalated... Casey Anthony was raised to lie. Sex abuse does things to us, it changes you... She's not guilty of murder. . . This is not a murder case. This is a sad, tragic accident that snowballed out of control."[3]

And with that, a seed was planted: Casey was the victim.

In total, the case of *The State of Florida v. Casey Marie Anthony* lasted six weeks, May to July 2011. It took thirty-three days of testimony, 400 pieces of evidence, and over ninety witnesses for the jury to reach a verdict that shocked and appalled the majority of America. Even though the defense team didn't present one shred of evidence that Casey was a victim of child sexual abuse and didn't demonstrate any alternatives as to how Caylee could have died, they were able to provide reasonable doubt that overshadowed all the circumstantial evidence submitted by the prosecution, often calling the prosecution's evidence "fantasy forensics."

As a result, on July 5, 2011, the jury of five men and seven women declared Casey "not guilty" on all the primary offenses: first degree, second degree, and third degree murder, aggravated child abuse, and aggravated manslaughter of a child. After everything, she was only convicted on four misdemeanor counts of providing false information to a law enforcement officer.

The Evolution of Tot Mom

The Casey Anthony trial wasn't just another murder case. It was a landmark event in American history that entirely captivated the nation. *Time* magazine dubbed it the "social media trial of the century." The *New York Post* wrote that the trial went "from being a newsworthy case to one of the biggest ratings draws in recent memory. When the verdict was delivered, CNN *Headline News* and CNN2, had its most watched hour in network history, peaking at 5.205 million viewers. A total of 142 million people listened on the radio or watched on TV as the jury acquitted Casey on the most severe counts. It quickly became the most publicized case in U.S. history, surpassing even the O.J. Simpson trial. "The Simpson case was the longest trial ever held in California, costing more than $20 million to fight and defend, running up 50,000 pages of trial transcript in the process. Reports say the Casey Anthony trial [far exceeded] these numbers."[4] Posts were coming in on Facebook so quickly that it was "too fast for all Facebook to even count them, meaning at least 10 per second."[5] MSNBC reported 325,283 Twitter posts on the day of the verdict, including numerous punches from celebrity folk:

> Rosanne Barr: "Kids only matter in this country when they are fetuses."
> Kim Kardashian: "What!!!!???!!!! CASEY ANTHONY FOUND NOT GUILTY!!!! I am speechless!"
> Carson Daly: "That jury better get into hiding."
> Joy Behar: "I am shocked by the #caseyanthonyverdict. Though I can't say this is the first time Florida screwed up an important vote. #HLN"
> Harvey Levin: "Having covered OJ Simpson…nothing really shocks me anymore, but this verdict really surprises me…especially how quickly it came."
> Sharon Osbourne: "Casey Anthony not guilty??.... It's a disgrace. She'll probably get her own reality show now."

Outside of the courtroom, it had been an easy case. Most felt that Casey was guilty. Common sense seemed to mount up against her, begging most to ask, "How could she not have done it?" The bulk of the legal pundits believed that even though it was only a case with circumstantial evidence, Casey would receive a guilty verdict. Jose Baez, the lead defense attorney, had a marked lack of trial experience in high profile criminal cases, resulting in horrible cross-examination of witnesses and distracting from the trial itself, unprepared as litigator in terms of questioning, leading the public and the media to belief that would be the downfall of the defense. So when the verdict rang in, people were outraged. Stunned. But truthfully to me—and those who really consider the facts—it wasn't shocking. America has a history, and it was in Casey's favor.

While there have been many cases where a guilty verdict has been based only on circumstantial evidence, this isn't often true in cases where women are charged with murdering their children. Mark Geragos, legendary criminal defense attorney who has defended the likes of Michael Jackson, Gary Condit, Susan McDougal, and Scott Peterson, would become the unpopular voice of legal reason when he concluded that there was no evidence as to the cause of death and, without that proof, Casey wouldn't be convicted of murder.

"I wasn't surprised with the verdict at all. I just think you're hard pressed to convict someone when you don't know the cause or manner of death. From the beginning, I thought the motive on the prosecution's side was silly ... to be free? That argument made no sense and the fact that the jury was sequestered allowed them to focus on the lack of evidence."[6]

Moreover, Geragos understood the key notion that juries are hard pressed to fully convict mothers. "I never thought Casey would get first-degree murder. First of all it's a mother and a daughter. Jurors are low to give death in these kinds of cases and number two you had her family members supporting her. Normally in a murder case you have the victims family screaming for blood and you didn't have that in this case and that makes a difference."[7]

In his interview with Dr. Phil, Geragos stated that Casey was acquitted by the unspoken norm of the "a pretty white girl exception." Although George was not on trial, in order to convict Casey of first-degree murder beyond a reasonable doubt, the prosecution would have had to disprove any allegations that he molested his daughter. The backlash of being labeled a child molester created an immediate bias amongst the jury towards George Anthony that fatally hurt his credibility. Overconfident, the prosecution failed to address the emotional impact that such an accusation would make with the jury.

With hubris, the prosecution presumed the jury would take George on his word and accept the judge's ruling of such allegations as inadmissible. Without hearing expert testimony to the contrary or revealing the finding of Casey's psychological evaluations, the prosecution did not disrupt the acts graphically described by defense attorney Jose Baez. In failing to do so, they put George on trial allowing for the jury to view Casey more sympathetically. This would allow the accusation to fester; it would be thrown out of court, but not out of the juror's minds.

Unlike the prosecution, Casey Anthony and her defense team sat directly across the room from all 12 jurors. The courtroom placement of Casey—conservatively and neatly dressed, with her hair pulled back to show an open view of her face and all her emotional reactions—would further provide the backlash of bias on the testimony given by George. An effective visual strategy in stark contrast to George seated throughout the trial in the back of the courtroom appearing stoic, reserved and unapproachable. Unfortunately, George's attempt to stay emotionally intact and preserve his dignity—while being accused of the most taboo act— would further add to the jury's questioning of his sincerity and integrity.

As a criminal defense attorney, Geragos stated, "Until you get past George, you're never going to convict her... it's just not going to happen."

In writing *Who Is Casey Anthony?*, my goal is to give you answers, to shed truth and light into a situation that is distinguished mostly by its darkness and lack of resolution. But this isn't just about Casey's guilt or innocence. Her ability to commit murder or not. It's about the larger cultural picture and insight into a very real but often overlooked reality: mothers who kill. Why do we, as a society, find it so difficult to believe that women—and more particularly mothers—can be culpable of such a despicable crime? Why can we not convict? Why do we see mothers only as mothers and not what they truly are: humans first, women second, and mothers third?

A Small Body of Evidence
Before we proceed through dissecting the Casey Anthony trial and what it indicates on a larger, social scale, it's essential to understand the basic facts of the case: who was involved and what was the evidence? By understanding Casey Anthony and her actions inside and out, we can understand more clearly the cultural phenomenon that's detrimentally entrenched in America.

The People to Solving the Puzzle
The trial was, in short, an exposé on the Anthony family. Throughout the case, very little attention was focused on any other suspects and, if so, the suspicions were quickly dismissed.

- **Casey Anthony** was admittedly an unlikely defendant. At twenty-two years old, with an attractive, appealing face, she hardly looked prepared for motherhood, much less murder.
- Casey's father, **George Anthony**, was a ten-year veteran homicide detective. The defense team accused George of molesting Casey at the tender age of eight years old,

arguing the abuse at the hands of her father caused her to act the way she did. Ultimately, George played the most pivotal role in the case.

- Casey's mother, **Cindy Anthony**, was a continual enabler of Casey's lies. Her desire in life was to be the perfect mother with the perfect family. She wanted to be perceived as the good mother and be loved by Casey. As a result, she was unable to truly parent.
- **Lee Anthony**, Casey's older brother, played a quieter role in the trial. He was Casey's Achilles heel.
- **Tony Lazarro** was Casey's boyfriend. During the thirty-one days Caylee was missing, Casey lived with Tony and spent a large portion of the time partying with him. At no point was he considered a suspect in the case.
- An unfortunate party to one of one of the many lies, Casey accused **Zenaida Fernandez-Gonzalez**– "Zanny the Nanny"–of acting as Caylee's nanny and then kidnapping her. These accusations were quickly disproved and dismissed.
- **Brian Burner** was the Anthony's neighbor and the individual Casey borrowed a shovel from.
- **Roy Kronk** was the utility worker who found Caylee's remains in the woods in August 2008, and wasn't viewed as credible. In November 2008, he contacted police again and in December 2008 Caylee's remains were verified. He was cleared of having any involvement in her murder.

Timeline of Events

- **August 9, 2005**

  Caylee is born. Prior to and in the early months of Casey's pregnancy, Casey tells her mother she is a "virgin." It is not until the fourth month of her pregnancy that Casey admits to her parents she is pregnant. The pregnancy continues to be hidden by Casey and her mother to Casey's brother, Lee, and all extended family members who have inquired.

- **March 17, 2008**

  At 2:43 p.m. there is a computer search done from the Anthony's home computer on neck breaking and how to make household products weapons.

- **March 21, 2008**

  At around 3:00 p.m., "How to make Chloroform" is searched on the Anthony's home computer. On both days, George, Cindy, and Lee have been confirmed by the prosecutors to be at work, leaving Casey as the only individual with access to the computer.

- **June 15, 2008**

  Cindy's mother, Shirley Pleasa, phones her daughter irate, that once again Casey has stolen a check from her grandfather's checkbook and purchased a cell phone for $354 at AT&T the same day. This is the last straw for Cindy, Casey's mother, who has made up her mind she is done with all of Casey antics. She will not tolerate any more excuses, deceit, and lack of responsibility from Casey. This is the day the straw broke the camel's back. It is important to note that for several months Cindy requested that Casey pay back the thousands of dollars she stole from her parents. Cindy spoke to a psychotherapist during the months leading up to

Caylee's disappearance. She was encouraged to contact child protective services to have Caylee taken from Casey. Cindy did not have the heart to follow through.

- **June 16, 2008**
  This is the last day Caylee is seen alive by her grandparents, George and Cindy Anthony, and likely the day that Caylee died. Casey and Caylee are last seen by George, Casey's father, leaving with individual back packs at 12:50 p.m. George spent the morning playing with Caylee and watching television while Casey dressed for work.

- **June 16, 2008**
  Casey and Caylee are last seen by George, Casey's father, leaving with individual back packs at 12:50 p.m. George spent the morning playing with Caylee and watching television. George leaves shortly after to go to work.

- **June 18, 2008**
  Casey borrows a shovel from her parents' neighbor, Brian Burner. She backs into her parents garage, an act Burner says he had never seen Casey do before. According to Burner, Casey returns the shovel an hour later.

- **June 19, 2008**
  Casey goes with Tony Lazzaro, her boyfriend, to help him look for an apartment.

- **June 20, 2008**
  Casey is captured in photos partying at a nightclub.

- **June 28, 2008**
  Casey's car is towed from the parking lot of a check-cashing store after being abandoned.

- **July 15, 2008**
  George picks up Casey's car from a tow yard. George and the attendant observe a strong odor emanating from the

vehicle; the smell of death. George calls Cindy regarding the smell. Later, back at the Anthony family home, Casey tells her brother, Lee Anthony, that she hasn't seen Caylee in a month and that a babysitter named Zanaida Fernandez Gonzalez (Zanny) kidnapped her. Cindy is walking through the hallway and overhears the confession.

- **July 15, 2008**
  Cindy Anthony, Casey's mother, calls 9-1-1, reporting Caylee's month-long disappearance. "There is something wrong," she says. "I found my daughter's car today [and] it smells like there's been a dead body in the damn car." Cindy knowingly finds the clothes Casey was last wearing on June 16, the last time Casey was seen on the floorboard in the back seat of the car. The pants smell like death the same as the car. Cindy takes the pants into the house and washes the pants, folds them, and leaves them on Casey's bed. She knowingly washes away any DNA or forensic evidence that may have told the story of Caylee's death.

- **July 15-16, 2008**
  Casey Anthony takes police to what she says is Zanny the Nanny's apartment, the last place she says she saw Caylee. It turns out to be a vacant apartment. Authorities also take her to Universal Studios where she said she worked, but supervisors say she hasn't worked there in more than two years.

- **July 16, 2008**
  Casey is arrested for child neglect, providing false information to investigators, and obstructing a criminal investigation. Bond is set at $500,000.

- **August 5, 2008**

  The State Attorney's Office files formal charges against Casey.

- **August 7, 2008**

  Investigators serve a search warrant at the Anthony home, and remove a number of clothing items belonging to Caylee, which Cindy said had been in Casey's car. Cindy had washed some of them because they had a "foul odor."

- **August 11, 2008**

  Roy Kronk, a utility worker, finds Caylee's remains. He says he went into the wooded area to urinate because, "We don't really have bathroom facilities." He calls the police several times in August regarding the remains, but the police don't see him as credible.

- **August 21, 2008**

  Leonard Padilla, a bounty hunter, posts Casey's $500,000 bail.

- **August 27, 2008**

  Air sample tests show that the trunk of Casey Anthony's car once held a decomposing human body.

- **August 29, 2008**

  Casey is arrested for a second time on charges of petty theft and falsifying checks. New bail is posted at $503,200.

- **September 3, 2008**

  Alleged Chloroform was found in the trunk of Casey's car.

- **September 24, 2008**

  Zenaida Fernandez-Gonzalez, the woman Casey named as Caylee's baby sitter, files a defamation lawsuit against Casey. Police had cleared Fernandez-Gonzalez earlier.

- **October 14, 2008**

  Casey is indicted on seven counts, including first-degree murder.

- **November 26, 2008**

  Investigators reveal that suspect terms were searched on the Internet on a computer that Casey accessed, including "neck breaking," "how to make chloroform," and "household weapons."

- **December 11, 2008**

  After being phoned again in November by Ray Krock, detectives find what they believe to be the remains of Caylee's body exactly where Ray Krock initially reported in Aug 2008.

- **December 19, 2008**

  Dr. Jan Garavaglia, a medical examiner, confirms that the remains are Caylee's.

- **January 21, 2009**

  According to reports released by the State Attorney General's Office, Caylee's mouth was covered with silver duct tape that wrapped around her head. It was adorned with a heart-shaped sticker.

- **January 23, 2009**

  George checks into a hotel with a six-pack of beer and mixture of tranquilizers and sleeping pills to kill himself. He phones family members. Family members become alarmed and George is hospitalized for reportedly trying to commit suicide.

- **April 13, 2009**

  Prosecutors decide to pursue the death penalty for Casey.

- **October 9, 2009**

  The state releases 1,400 pages of documents in the case, including photos of Casey's "La Bella Vida" tattoo, meaning "Beautiful Life" in Italian. Casey allegedly got the tattoo during the time her daughter was missing.

- **December 18, 2009**
  Judge Stan Strickland rejects the defense's request to remove the death penalty. Casey is accused of going on a "spending spree" while Caylee was still missing in summer 2008 with the money she stole from her parents savings.
- **January 26, 2010**
  Casey pleads guilty to thirteen counts of check-fraud.
- **March 6, 2010**
  Prosecution releases letters between Casey and a fellow inmate. Anthony allegedly reveals details about the crime that only Caylee's killer would know.
- **March 8, 2010**
  It's announced the trial will begin May 9, 2011.
- **March 19, 2010**
  The judge declares Casey as indigent, meaning taxpayers will pay for her defense.
- **April 19, 2010**
  Judge Strickland recuses himself. Judge Belvin Perry, Jr. takes over.
- **April 26, 2011**
  Judge Perry rules that the prosecution may present "controversial" evidence to the jury, including an FBI analyst to testify regarding the heart-shaped sticker found on Caylee, a K-9 unit handler to talk about a dog's findings near the trunk of Casey's car, and the state to discuss a strand of hair found in Casey's trunk that is said to come from a decomposing body.
- **July 15, 2010**
  Judge Perry rules that Cindy's 9-1-1 call may be used in trial.

- **May 9, 2011**

  Jury selection begins.

- **May 24, 2011**

  The trial begins. In opening statements, the prosecution argues Casey knocked-out her daughter using chloroform, duct-taped her mouth shut, and tossed her body in the woods. Defense lawyer Jose Baez claimed that Caylee Anthony accidentally drowned in the family swimming pool while home with Casey and Casey's father, George. Next, he claimed the reason Casey reacted so strangely to her daughter's death was that she had been abused as a child by her father. George Anthony denies these allegations.

- **June 10, 2011**

  Casey breaks down when John J. Schultz, a professor of anthropology, testified about the condition of Caylee's remains. He told the court that Caylee's bones had been chewed on by wild animals.

  June 23, 2011

  Cindy claims she was the one who Google-searched "chloroform" to figure out whether the chemical "chlorophyll" in bamboo was making her dog tired.

- **July 1, 2011**

  Prosecutors bring in Cindy's co-workers to testify that Casey's mother was working and could not have been at home to Google-search those items.

- **July 3, 2011**

  Closing arguments occur.

- **July 5, 2011**

  After over ten hours of deliberations, the jury deems Casey not guilty of murder, aggravated child abuse, and

manslaughter, but guilty of providing false information to
investigators. Sentencing is scheduled for July 7.

- **July 7, 2011**
  Judge Belvin Perry sentences Casey Anthony to maximum
  one year in prison for each of four counts of lying to law
  enforcement, plus a $1,000 fine for each count. The total
  fine is $4,618 including court costs to be repaid at $20
  monthly beginning in February 2012.

- **July 17, 2011**
  Casey Anthony is released from the Orange County Jail in
  Orlando Florida after being credited with 1,043 previous
  days in jail, plus good behavior while behind bars.

Tracing Casey's Movements

Florida's *Local 6 News* investigative reporter Tony Pipitone did further
investigation by tracing Casey's whereabouts using her cell phone
records. Through this method, Pipitone was able to determine what
cell phone towers Casey's phone pinged while Casey was missing,
narrowing the possibilities of where Casey could have been and what
she could have been doing.[8]

According to Michael Bouldin, a criminal defense attorney
in northern Kentucky:

> *The technology allows a cellular telephone company to track
> a person based on their travels in real time. In hindsight, the
> pings come from a specific tower when a call or text is made
> or received by the owner of a cellular telephone.*
>
> *According to cNET, Mobile devices, when they are
> within range, constantly let cell towers and the mobile
> switching center, which is connected to multiple towers,
> know of their location. The mobile switching center uses*

the location information to ensure that incoming calls and messages are routed to the tower nearest to the user...

When someone is missing, even this small bit of information can prove useful in determining the approximate location of a device using the updates from the mobile switching center. If the mobile subscriber is still within cell phone range, authorities can track his or her general movement by following the sequence of towers the phone has contacted or pinged. And if the cell phone goes out of range or runs out of battery power, the mobile operator may be able to use the last recorded location before the cell phone either lost its signal or lost power.

But the most useful information for locating people when they are lost comes when someone has initiated or received a call or text message on their phone. Mobile operators keep records of these events for billing purposes in what is known as a call data record, or CDR. And they can go back to these records to get a historical account of the cell phone's location.[9]

According to Pipitone, Casey's phone pinged twenty different cell phone towers 754 times between June 16, the last day Caylee was seen alive, and June 30, the day Casey's car was found abandoned. Each of the 754 pings indicated that her phone had received or sent a call or text message. The majority of the pings—97 percent—were to one of four places: her boyfriend's apartment near Winter Park, her friend's home in Orlando, her parents' home off Chickasaw Trail, or the Fusion nightclub.

Following the cell phone records in conjunction with witness accounts, on Monday, June 16, George saw Casey and Caylee leave his house at 1:50 p.m. Casey reports to George that she is dropping Caylee off with Zanny the Nanny and heading to work at Universal. That afternoon, Casey made three calls that accessed towers surrounding the immediate area of the Anthony house. She made a fourteen minute call to her boyfriend, Tony Lazzaro, at 1:00 p.m. Shortly after, at 1:44 p.m., she spoke with her best friend, Amy Huizenga, for thirty-six minutes. At 2:52, she spoke with her ex-fiance, Jesse Grund, for eleven minutes.

But at 4:11 p.m., Casey began trying to reach her mother, Cindy, making four attempts in two minutes. Cindy was not to be disturbed as she was in a meeting. On the fourth call, Cindy steps out of the meeting to speak to Casey. Cindy is annoyed and tells Casey she will speak to her later. Casey does not disclose what is so important to call so many times. Casey then traveled north from her parents' home and called her boyfriend for one minute at 4:19 p.m. Two minutes later, she talked to Grund for a minute, and tried to call her mother again at 4:25 p.m. There was no other communication from Casey's cell phone until a call was made to her boyfriend's apartment at 5:57 p.m. Two hours later, Anthony and Lazzaro were captured on surveillance video at a Blockbuster, renting a movie that contains a scene of a rotting body in a car trunk. It is Casey who specifically chooses the movie for the evening's entertainment.

On June 17, Casey returned to her parents' home around 2:30 p.m. At 4:00 p.m., her phone pinged a tower southwest of the house near Lee Vista Boulevard and South Goldenrod Road, an area where Equusearch volunteers searched for Caylee. At 5:20 p.m., a tower was pinged near Blanchard Park, another site searched in August by Equusearch. Casey's cell phone went silent from 5:23 p.m. until 8:23 p.m. when her cell phone pinged a tower near her boyfriend's apartment. By then, around 8:30 p.m. on Tuesday, June 17, Caylee had not been seen alive for nearly a day and a half.

While some of her movements had thus far been suspicious, it's important to remember that the chemical evidence in the trunk of Casey's car indicates that the decomposing body was there up to two and a half days after death, so anyone searching for Caylee's body had to ask: Where did Casey go next?

On Wednesday June 18, Casey borrowed a shovel from the next-door neighbor, who witnessed her backing into her parents' car garage. The neighbor remembers this because Casey always pulls in headfirst. Cell phone pings indicate that Casey was at or near her parents' home from 2:30-3:30 p.m. Anthony's phone later pinged a different spot near the Econ Trail, south of Lake Underhill—another location detectives guided Equsearch volunteers to look for signs of Caylee's body. Scientific evidence suggests that a body left its chemical signature in the trunk of Anthony's car after decomposing for less than two and a half days, which would be about the same time period between the aforementioned cell phone pings. Circumstantial, but interesting.

Later that day, Casey and her boyfriend are seen on surveillance video visiting the Blockbuster store near his apartment on University Boulevard. Caylee is not in the video. Casey's boyfriend told *Local 6 News* that he had not seen Caylee at that point for two weeks, leading investigators to believe that Caylee may have died on June 16.

At Blockbuster, Casey and her boyfriend rented two movies, one of which was *Untraceable*—a choice that becomes even more disturbing once you consider the location of where Caylee's body may have been. The movie shows an FBI agent pursued by a sadistic cyber-stalker who pops the trunk of a car and is overcome by the smell of a fly-infested, rotting corpse that was left there by the killer. Investigators believe Caylee's body was left in the trunk of her mother's car, where it decomposed, emitting an odor.

Reasonable Doubt

The nation struggled on both an emotional and intellectual level when the verdict came in. America's judicial system requires prosecutors to prove their case beyond a reasonable doubt. The jury system determines, based upon the evidence presented in court, whether or not the prosecution has proved its case beyond a reasonable doubt. With this in mind, it's hard to be surprised by the outcome. Keep in mind, juries who are sequestered do not see the evidence inadmissible in court. They also do not hear the interviews the public is privy to through the media with those intimately involved in the case. They hear only what the witnesses answer to specific questions by both the defense and prosecution. Jurors often do not hear what the witness would like to say to complete their answer. Without Casey taking the stand, it was extremely difficult to convict her of first or second-degree murder, because there was no hard evidence. Supported further in the timeline above, there was:

- No evidence as to the cause of death.
- No blood evidence in the trunk of the car or anywhere.
- No DNA evidence on the remains, or any of the items buried with Caylee.
- No evidence of blunt force trauma to Caylee's skull.
- No fractures or breaks in Caylee's bones.
- No tissue on Caylee's skeleton that can suggest bludgeoning, stabbing, shooting, or strangulation.
- No evidence of being beaten to death.
- No prior hospitalizations for physical abuse.
- No murder weapon.
- Not enough Chorlyphil in the trunk to determine if it was from a household cleaning product that anyone might have vs. Casey making it on her own.

- No evidence that Chorophyll was in fact used on Caylee at all.
- No lung tissue to determine if Caylee died of an accidental drowning in the pool, or evidence as to whether or not Casey murdered her in the pool by drowning her.
- All DNA on clothes Casey wore that day were washed off by Cindy.
- No footprints in the woods that matched Casey or evidence on her shoes.

A computer search performed three months prior to Caylee's death is a long jump to committing premeditated murder. In other words, there can be a time when a person was triggered, thought about and researched it, however they may have decided against it. I believe the initial trigger for Casey was the change in her mother Cindy. Cindy began speaking to Casey more aggressively holding her more accountable, paying attention to money missing and the use of her credit cards. Cindy began to face reality that George was right that Casey had been lying and that she had never worked at the sporting goods store part-time to take care of Caylee.

Esteemed forensic anthropologist, Kathy Reichs, couldn't find any evidence of murder on Caylee's skeletal remains. Nor could esteemed forensic scientist Dr. Lee, who was called on the Laci Peterson, Jon Benet Ramsey, and Nicole Brown Simpson's cases. From purely a legal perspective there was simply no way to prove whether Caylee's death was accidental, pre-meditated murder, second-degree murder, or aggravated manslaughter. Looking at the third charge of aggravated child abuse, the not-guilty verdict was a little more shocking. Throughout the trial, the defense kept floating the story of an accidental drowning so much that it seemed impossible she wouldn't be convicted of at least that much. If Caylee died in the pool, then there is an issue of child neglect and if George was indeed at the house when Caylee died why did no one mention what he was doing at the time of her death. Two adults in the house and neither one could hear a child drowning in the pool, especially when the glass sliding door was left ajar for the dog to come in and out. But aggravated child abuse means the prosecution had to prove, beyond a reasonable doubt, that a) there was an accident and b) it resulted from Casey's negligent care, even though the defense claimed Caylee died in the pool.

At the end of the trial, the only thing the prosecution could prove without reasonable doubt was that Casey lied to law enforcement—a measly four counts of misdemeanor. Very hard to swallow, I know, when everything surrounding this case is glaring.

Nancy Grace, who knew the Casey Anthony trial inside and out, said, "I had to take reams of notes to keep up with the scientific evidence as it came in… The jurors very rarely took notes they took notes for neither side…. you know that's a problem…. they were overwhelmed by the evidence, they did not understand the scientific evidence…and I also think it's very, very confusing evidence."

As Grace keys in on, the defense's greatest ally was confusion. Well known for her lies and deceit, Casey and her defense team led the jury down a path of an unbelievable story, clogging up the minds and understanding of the jurors. While Casey's lies in the moment are neither clever nor smart, she is calculating and cold to the core, a dangerous manipulator of the truth. As we'll discuss in later chapters, Casey wins not by the quality of her lies, but the quantity of them, creating so much doubt that it's hard to pick your way through to the truth. Moreover, if you're the one who is trying to hold her accountable for her actions, she'll go in for the kill. In the case of Caylee's alleged murder, she used her father, George, to create reasonable doubt. And while the prosecution tried to discredit Casey and the stories told, the damage was done.

We can sort through all of the evidence and all of the facts that have been presented to try to come up with a cohesive argument, but the fact of the matter is there are people in the world who are capable of committing and covering up the cold-blooded murder of their child. And even though we might have an instinct and even though that instinct might be right, without admissible evidence, and a less complicated presentation of the case that any juror can follow, an American jury will not convict a young attractive mother for first-degree murder.

Chapter Two
The American Phenomenon: Mothers Who Kill

It's an unsettling reality, one that demonstrates the worst in human kind. And yet for something so appalling, it's markedly common. According to the World Health Organization in 2009, one person is murdered every sixty seconds.[10] That's 86,400 murders a day.

And while murder in all its faces is awful, the worst is often considered to be mothers who murder their children. In these horrible situations, those who are to be the ultimate caretakers become the ultimate dangers, taking away the very thing they gave. For most of us, the thought of murder is unfathomable, and the thought of killing our children even more so. Lord Astor, a British philanthropist, put it this way: "Everyone starts out totally dependent on a woman. The idea that she could turn out to be your enemy is terribly frightening."[11] And with this societal view of women, there comes an unrealistic and fully engrained belief that mothers—and in this case, Casey Anthony—can do no wrong.

The term "human nature" is frequently used in psychology, sociology, and philosophy to describe the myriad of behaviors found in the human race—a breed of animals capable of anything and the ability to cover-up anything. But when we learn of the heinous crimes of mothers who kill their children, we don't want to believe it; we can't believe it. Cold-blooded women who murder their children are not encompassed within our definition of "human nature." We can more easily wrap our minds around "The Milwaukee Cannibal" serial killer, Jeffrey Dahmer, killing and dismembering seventeen young black, and other minority boys and men. Or yet the case of "The Grim Sleeper serial killer—an African American male who is responsible for killing at least ten individuals over a period of two decades—than we can accept a mother killing her child.

But despite how incomprehensible the action seems, women are entirely capable of committing heinous and violent acts, including killing and harming their children. Moreover, there's a precedent in history that women murder their children for reasons just as selfish as men: they want the insurance *money*; they have fallen in *love* and want to stay with their new man who doesn't want children; the financial security provided by their husband has diminished; they're used to the "good life" and believe that by getting rid of their children they'll have money to maintain their current *lifestyle*; they want to dominate over the father of the child by using the child as an object they possess and is theirs to do what they wish to assert their *power*. But despite what research and history says, we're hard-pressed to believe the culpability of women. Instead, we'd rather believe that— if this horrible action does happen—it's in the hysterical heat of the moment, a pure accident. In other words, Mom "snapped."

The question is: why do we have different expectations for women and men when it comes to violent and lethal behavior? How can our perceptions inform reality? And how did all of this factor into the Casey Anthony case?

Parental Killing

To clearly understand the actions of women, we first must understand the act itself. Filicide is the intentional act of a parent killing his or her child, and it's a deed seen in the majority of countries around the world, among every social class, from poor to wealthy. While filicide isn't necessarily a widespread occurrence, it is the leading cause of child death in developed countries. In a poll of twenty-five countries, the homicide rate for children under one year old known as infanticide, the killing of an infant was higher than the rate for adult homicide.

Suzanne Barnard, a social worker with the children's division of the American Humane Association, says, "I don't think most parents who murder children wake up in the morning and say, 'This is the day I'm going to kill my kids.'"[12]

Dewey Cornell, a clinical psychologist at the University of Virginia, continues the thought, saying, "Usually one thing leads to another, and the problem escalates to the point where eventually the person caves in under the pressure and stress."[13]

"Generally parents who kill their children tend to be under a lot of stress. They may be very young and not ready for the demands of parenthood. In all likelihood, they are socially isolated and do not have a large social net. They may have been victims of violence themselves," says Susan Hiatt, the director of the Kempe National Center for the Prevention and Treatment of Child Abuse and Neglect in Denver.[14]

At the same time, while stress and the well-known concept of the straw that broke the camel's back are very realistic, many times there are indicators, signs and warnings that certain parents can be predisposed to violent acts or the ability to "snap."

Jill Korbin, an anthropology professor at Case Western Reserve University, says murder "is usually not the first assault on the child. These women often let others know about incidents of abuse prior to the fatal incident. But many times, the seriousness of the incident isn't recognized."[15]

Palm Beach County assistant state attorney Scott Cupp, who heads the Crimes Against Children Unit, says: "We're burying too many kids who died at the hands of their parents. We need to be taking more of them out of these homes before this happens. I'm tired of it, sick of it. A lot of these kids could have been saved. Yet so often society doesn't pay attention to the signs."[16]

The truth is, parenting is one of the most demanding and significant jobs in the world today. And yet it's one that requires no training, no job application, and even no desire. Some parents are unfit and unwilling; they let their selfish desires rise above their parental obligations, and children become the victims.

As Steve Pinker says, "It happens in families where there's no history of violence and where there's a long history of violence. It crosses racial lines, socioeconomic lines. It's not black, Hispanic or white, rich or poor. It's a horror that we as a society are going to be confronted with again and again."[17]

Filicide is simply one of the most prevalent and tragic problems in the world today.

Fathers Who Kill

When we study violence and murder, research is typically—and expectedly—focused on men. Men are believed to be the more destructive, violence-prone gender, entirely capable of gruesome and deadly acts. Women pale in comparison. They are seen as defenseless and innocent, universally deemed the nurturing gatekeepers of the home. However, as Patrice Pearson, a prominent crime researcher, notes in her book *When She Was Bad*, "Women commit the majority of child homicides in the U.S., a greater share of physical child abuse, an equal rate of sibling violence and assaults on the elderly, about a quarter of child sexual abuse, an overwhelming share of the killing of newborns, and a fair preponderance of spousal assaults. The question is: how do we come to perceive what girls and women do? Violence is still universally considered to be the province of the male. Violence is masculine. Men are the cause of it, and women and children are the ones who suffer."[18]

The majority of society continues to judge female violence by what women are supposed to be like rather than how they really are. But lower visibility of women's violent crimes—in both research and the media—should not overwhelm the truth of how deadly and sadistic women can be.

In order to fully understand how society perceives women who murder, in particular mothers, we must understand how society perceives fathers who kill, as well. How are they typically convicted? How are men treated differently than women? How are their motivations different? How are they the same?

In an article by Katherine Ramsland on "Fathers Who Kill," she lists the various reasons men commit murder. While some men, such as Scott Peterson, kill because they simply don't want to be a father, most are driven for specific, emotional reasons:[19]

- Losing control over the family circumstances/panic over powerlessness
- Seeing only adverse circumstances ahead in life/ desperation/frustration
- Feeling overwhelmed and unable to let the family live while he dies

- Seeing the deaths as a necessary sacrifice
- Believing the children cannot survive without him
- Revenge against an estranged wife, or teaching her a lesson
- Grief over losing the family in a divorce
- Discipline gone too far
- Possessiveness/entitlement/ownership
- Psychosis
- Self-enrichment
- Projecting their self-hatred onto the children
- Killing witnesses to abuse
- A joint crime with the mother—erasing the family
- Compassion
- Duty to the family
- Suicide by proxy
- Jealousy of children who are getting involved with others
- Difficulty adjusting to being a parent
- A long tradition of abuse in the family that just continues
- The idea that children must serve the parent's needs

Out of all of these, there are four driving reasons for the ultimate crime: lifestyle, power, love, and money—the ultimate of which is power. And while both sexes do murder for power, the key difference is women murder their children to *gain* power while men murder their children due to a *loss* of power and the loss of feeling in control.

"It takes a special power to kill a fellow man and it gives you a secret something—a confidence, afterward. Maybe you are more of a philosopher than I am," says an interviewed Moscow hit man.

"When you fly, at take-off, there is a strange feeling in your body, not explicable, but strange. A sort of revolution in your belly. That's the way I feel when I kill. It's no mystery."[20]

By murdering, men find themselves momentarily in control once again of situations that spiraled out of their hands. Consider the example of Dr. Anthony Paul. The forty-nine year old physician believed there was no alternative for his family. His wife, Malanie, was forty-eight years old and suffered severely from arthritis and depression. His seventeen-year-old daughter, Medhini, was developmentally disabled and unable to care for herself. Instead of enduring life and its hardships, Dr. Paul decided he would "provide" mercy by killing his family together through lethal injection. He didn't even spare his twelve-year-old son, Anthony, fearing that he would be placed in a foster home and deemed a misfit. By murdering his wife, daughter, and son, he could heal his family and control the situation.

Or when they have recently been laid off and can no longer financially provide for their families. They are emotionally fragile, have low frustration tolerance, and extremely poor coping strategies.

In 1989, a business owner, Robert Lynch, lost his business and went into debt. When his wife became pregnant with their fourth child, he couldn't handle the additional load, so he shot every member of his family and then committed suicide.

In a similar case of financial powerlessness, in 1994, Bruce Sweazy was laid off. He got an antidepressant for his suicidal tendencies, but ultimately didn't take them. Instead he murdered his wife, killing her and their sons with an axe before killing himself with a gunshot to the chest.

These men, such as Robert Lynch and Bruce Sweazy's self-worth was dependent upon external factors; the ability to provide for their family and keep up with the Jones. They live beyond their means purchasing cars and homes while living on credit. Feeling that they are a failure, they murder their family to save face from further embarrassment.

Professor Jack Levin, an expert at Northeastern University in Boston, Massachusetts, agrees, "The profile of a family annihilator is a middle-aged man, a good provider who would appear to neighbors to be a dedicated husband and a devoted father... often he tends to be quite isolated. He is often profoundly dedicated to his family, but has few friends of his own or a support system outside the family. He will have suffered some prolonged frustration and feelings of inadequacy, but when he suffers some catastrophic loss it is usually financial or the loss of a relationship. He doesn't hate his children, but he often hates his wife and blames her for his miserable life. He feels an overwhelming sense of his own powerlessness. He wants to execute revenge and the motive is almost always to 'get even.'"[21]

Men most often kill their children for *revenge*. These men are possessive and feel a sense of entitlement. Those who knew them outside of the home will say, "I can't believe it!" However, inside the home they are verbally and emotionally abusive. It is not uncommon to find a history of domestic violence. They are unable to individuate themselves from those closest to them. In turn, they project their self-hate on the mother of their children. Feelings of powerlessness become uncontrollable when the woman divorces them and wants custody of the kids. These men seek *revenge* against their ex-spouse to permanently make her feel the severity of their abandonment and loss of control. The child is used as the object of their revenge, "I will kill what you love the most and you will suffer for the rest of your life."

All in all, the male murder is not a tough nut to crack. Being the dominant sex in most societies, we can understand—on an emotional and intellectual level—how a father's feeling of inadequacy or desire for revenge can result in violent action. It isn't pretty or pleasing, but it's believable.

But what about the flipside of the coin? When it's a woman's neck in the noose, do we see things differently? As clearly? Does our perception line up with reality? And what perception does the media present us with?

Mothers in the Media

People are revolted by women who murder their children—and rightly so. But the action is not nearly as scarce as we might like to believe and the reasons not nearly so clean cut or excusable. According to the American Anthropological Association, in the United States, three to five children a day are killed by their parents.[22] Out of those, two hundred women per year kill their children.

As Jill Korbin, an expert on child abuse says, even though homicide is one of the leading causes of death for children under the age of four, we still "persist with the unrealistic view that this is rare behavior."[23] Moreover, when cases of child murder are reported to the wider national audience, the perpetrator is often the father. Statistically, women's crimes are hardly as documented or ridiculed as men's.

According to Patricia Pearson, "Women commit the majority of child homicides in the United States, a greater share of physical child abuse, an equal rate of sibling violence and assaults on the elderly, about a quarter of child sexual abuse, an overwhelming share of the killings of newborns, and a fair preponderance of spousal assaults. . . The sole explanation offered by criminologists for violence committed by a woman is that it is involuntary, the rare result of provocation or mental illness, as if half the population of the globe consisted of saintly stoics who never succumbed to fury, frustration, or greed. Though the evidence may contradict the statement, the consensus runs deep. Women from all walks of life, at all levels of power—corporate, political, of familial, women in combat and on police forces—have no part in violence. It is one of the most abiding myths of our time."[24]

Consider, for example, Jane Toppan. In 1885, she was a nurse at Cambridge Hospital where she used her patients as opportunities for experiments. "This is my ambition," she said, "to have killed more people, more helpless people, than any man or woman has ever killed."[25] She was convicted of poisoning over 100 patients in a nursing home, murdering many of those as a result of her actions. However, she was declared not guilty by reason of insanity. Despite the scale of Toppan's crime, she went down to very little acclaim. Shortly prior to her actions, Jack the Ripper murdered five prostitutes in London, claiming the headlines.

In 2000, President Bill Clinton launched the 5 billion dollar funding for the Violence Against Women Act. He referenced statistics of how a woman was beaten every twelve seconds, resulting in approximately 900,000 women beaten per year. However, he didn't mention the flip side of the coin, noting that 835,000 men were victims of domestic violence, as well.

The founder of the first women's shelter, Erin Pizzey, received violent threats when she began looking for ways to help men who suffer from beatings from their wives and girlfriends. She now has to have a police escort for public speaking because of the potential dangerous backlash.

"There is now an established domestic violence industry which fears any acknowledgement of the well-established scientific fact that women can be as violent as men with their intimate partners. . . Because of these views, and daring to speak out, I've been vilified and physically threatened many times by women in the domestic violence movement. Don't tell me women can't be violent! Nowadays, you won't even find my name or my domestic violence books mentioned in the established domestic violence literature. . . I've been erased because of heresy, for daring to speak the truth."[26]

The problem here is not that the media focuses too much on violence done to women and children by men; all violence and murder committed is wrong and should be documented, researched, and actively prevented. The bigger issue is society's inability to accurately report the violent and lethal behaviors of women, as well. Without being realistic about what all human beings are capable of, we will continue to be susceptible to the worst.

"The consequences of our refusal to concede female contributions to violence are manifold. It affects our capacity to promote ourselves as autonomous and responsible beings," says Pearson. "It affects our ability to develop a literature about ourselves that encompasses the full array of human emotions and experience. It demeans the right our victims have to be valued. And it radically impedes our ability to recognize dimensions of power that have nothing to do with formal structures of patriarchy. Perhaps, above all, the denial of women's aggression profoundly undermines our attempt as a culture to understand violence, to trace its causes and to quell them."[27]

Perception is Everything
One of the largest reasons society has a hard time conceding women's role in violence is physical perception. It's a fact of life that we like people to look the part and, when they don't, we have a hard time accepting it.

Imagine it this way. It's the start of football season and your favorite team takes the field. When the new running back is announced, you can't believe what you're seeing. Out walks a 5'6, 170 pound man. This can't possibly be right, you're thinking. Comparatively, he's tiny. And yet, by the end of the game, he's scored two touchdowns. Even though he didn't look the part, he certainly could play it. It's something you had to see to believe.

In the Casey Anthony case, perception was everything. Casey was a young, attractive, white, middle-class female. We expected her to behave a certain way because of how she looked, and the accusations against her didn't appropriately align with our pre-conceived beliefs. Even though she was capable of murder, had the means and the motivation, we find ourselves predisposed to doubt because she looked more like a neighbor than a ruthless killer.

In closing arguments, the prosecution asked one of the most poignant questions: Who benefits most with Caylee gone? Did Casey have a motive for killing her daughter? Did anyone else? If we emotionally remove ourselves from the case and evaluate purely based on the evidence, the answer seems clear. No one stood to gain more from Caylee's absence than Casey. And no one stood in the way of the truth more than Casey. She lied, misled, and—most pointing of all—never sought true justice for her daughter. But as a nation, we sat riveted to the TV screen still not sure we could believe that a young, pretty, middle class, white mother could kill her baby girl.

A question we have to ask ourselves is, how would the case have been different if it had been a man—Caylee's father—who didn't report her missing for thirty-one days? There is no doubt in my mind that even with only circumstantial evidence, the father would have been convicted on one of the three counts of murder. Too much common sense shouts, "Guilty!" And yet when it comes to women, we falter in our convictions. Even though women can be as ruthless as men and have proven to be cold-blooded killers, we pause, hoping that we are wrong and must simply be missing a piece of the equation.

The overall perception of mothers isn't only off kilter when it comes to violence, though; it's misinterpreted on a number of levels, drastically affecting how women treat themselves, their children, and their spouses.

In a recent survey of over 24,000 women taken by the *Today* show's Women's Blog and Parenting.com found:

- More than 30% of mothers use their jobs as an *excuse* to avoid having to care for their children.
- 53% say they would rather have a night of uninterrupted sleep versus a night of sex.
- 23% miss their alone time most.
- 18% have medicated their children for a long car ride or plane ride.
- 8% medicate their children regularly to sleep.
- 14% miss their pre-baby body.
- 13% miss spontaneity.
- 44% would rather be thinner than their kids be smarter.
- 42% would rather have more money than spending time with their kids.
- 1 in 5 missed their life before children.
- 33% lie about their parenting practices to their friends, family, and other mothers; and
- 87% say they judge other moms.

Outside of the 87 percent of moms who judge other moms, Dr. Nancy Snyderman, the *Today* show's medical correspondent, made it very clear that she believes "the figures are way too low" and a huge number of mothers who took the survey were "fibbing." Dr. Snyderman and others instrumental in the survey agree that "there is a universal exhaustion among women" and women are fearful of being "perceived as selfish."

But these feelings, even if somewhat selfish, are entirely natural. And exhaustion, frustration, isolation, and lack of support from others can lead even the best of moms to become unknowingly neglectful, as well as physically or emotionally abusive toward their children. And those small actions of neglect—such as over-medicating a child—can lead to far more drastic repercussions, such as brain damage in a child or accidental death.

These feelings are all indicators that mothers are begging for an opportunity to be human; they want to express their concerns without judgment so they can get the support they need and develop new coping strategies. They are seeking balance in their life; they want to find a way to be a parent, but still maintain their identity.

On the other hand, of course, there is a truth many don't like to acknowledge: some women simply aren't made to be mothers. Many women simply don't want to have children at all and, if they do become pregnant, they opt for abortion or adoption. Consider this: one in three women under the age of forty has an abortion. So what are the chances that some women who don't want to be mothers actually end up with a child? Terrifyingly high.

On a certain level, we take the maternal instinct for granted. We want to believe its part of a female's DNA. And while most mothers do recognize and perform the obligations of motherhood—and often with joy—other women choose not to. At the end of the day, there are simply some mothers who don't know how to perform the role and there are others who simply don't want to. And when this happens—either out of ignorance or selfishness—children are the victims. And in the worst cases, death is a result.

How a woman sees herself and her role in the family is a societal crisis of epidemic proportions. These are not petty, emotional, whining problems of women, but true triggers for tragedy.

Consider Angela Thompson. In 1983, in Sacramento, California, Angela believed God was instructing her to kill her child, telling her that her nine-month old baby boy was the devil. So she drowned him in the bathtub. "I thought if I killed the baby that my husband would raise him to life again in three days and that the world would know that my husband was Jesus Christ," she explains. "When he was dead, I thought his face was contorted like the devil's."[28]

Or consider Michele Remington, a young woman from Bennington, Vermont who shot her six-week old son with a .22 caliber handgun. Or Kathleen Householder from West Virginia who grew tired of her two-week-old daughter's fussing and hit her over the head with a rock and then dumped her in the river.

As a society, we have created a myth that mothers are blameless, and the culture of 2011 still has difficulty coming to terms with women behaving in male-defined aggressive patterns. Mothers, particularly in our Judeo-Christian-based society, are held as sacred symbols. Mother's Day is one of the most nationally recognized days on the American calendar. Sons and daughters have brunches and lunches; they buy flowers, make breakfast in bed, and write thoughtful cards. Children who don't recognize the day are labeled as "angry," "disrespectful," "lacking loyalty," "selfish," or "unloving." A mother can commit the most egregious abuse on her children, and society still blindly pressures sons and daughters, regardless of age, to "forgive" their mother with such statements as, "But it's your mother!" or, "You only have one mother." And it's these very myths of motherhood and mother love that make people like Casey Anthony so difficult to convict.

Peg Streep, author of *Mean Mothers*, was quoted by abcnews. go.com as saying, "I was personally shocked by the verdict... Ultimately the myths of motherhood—combined with the descriptions of Casey as a good mother and the photos of a smiling baby with her mom—apparently proved more convincing than the evidence the prosecution presented... In a world where every other kind of love is conditional, people cling to the myth of mother love—and, of course, the myth renders the act of killing a child you've birthed, fed, dressed, and cuddled with unthinkable... There was plenty of evidence Casey did all of [these] things, even with care."[29]

We've come to the point where gender differences created by society have unfairly polluted our perception of women and what they are and are not capable of. We need to re-educate ourselves to accept that murder and mayhem are not solely male conditions but, in fact, are human conditions. Our current human conditioning tells us women do not kill their children because, if that were true, then anything is is possible and we are left with total lack of emotional and physical security. Who will protect us from harm if not our mother? But with victims like two-year-old Caylee Anthony on our hands, we have no time to waste. Even if it isn't pretty or how we would like it, we must start seeing the world clearly now.

Chapter Three
No Room for Excuses

One of the most public cases of maternal filicide was Andrea Yates. In 2001, Andrea drowned her five children in the bathtub of her home. She was convicted of capital murder and sentenced to life in prison with the possibility of parole in forty years. However, the judgment was overturned in 2006 when the conviction was appealed and a Texas jury deemed Andrea not guilty by reason of insanity. Prior to "snapping," Andrea had been suffering for some time with severe postpartum depression and postpartum psychosis, had tried to commit suicide, and had been hospitalized. The jury believed Andrea was not fully aware of or in control of her actions.

In cases where women murder their children, we want to believe insanity and mental disorders play a significant role. Those are the only explanations that we—as a society who by and large exalts motherhood—can swallow. Otherwise, how could a mother's disregard for her children possibly be explained? As the world followed the Casey Anthony trial, our instinct was to make excuses for her. How else could we justify a mother who parties for thirty-one days straight while her daughter is missing? How could we explain away Casey's lack of concern and her tapestry of lies?

In turn, we asked the obvious: Could Casey, like Andrea, suffer from chronic mental illnesses? Could there be a reason other than pure selfishness and a complete lack of disregard for human life? Even if Casey didn't murder her daughter, her actions surrounding Caylee's disappearance are despicable.

What in the world, we have to ask, is wrong with her?

Fit for Trial

Historically, mental stability has played a key role in the cases of women who commit murder.

Consider the below:

In 2009, Jenny Lizette Erazo-Rodriguez, an illegal immigrant from Honduras, strangled her four-year-old daughter, and attempted to kill her six-year-old daughter, believing God told her to do so. Erazo-Rodriguez was found not guilty by reason of insanity and was committed to a state psychiatric facility.

In another case in 2009, police found a three-week old baby boy, Scott Wesley Sanchez Buchholz, dead and mutilated in his family's home. His mother, Otty Sanchez, a thirty-four year old woman in Texas, brutally killed her son, eating part of his brain. The defense came to an agreement with the prosecution without having to go to trial, and Sanchez was found not guilty by reason of insanity. Similarly, in 2000, a thirty-eight year old woman, Janice Taylor, stabbed her five-year-old son twenty seven times, claiming he was "evil." Amazingly, her son survived the incident and Taylor was found not guilty by reason of insanity.

Dr. Phillip Resnick, an expert in child killings, conducted a study in 1969, which found that mothers convicted of murdering their children were hospitalized 68 percent of the time and imprisoned 27 percent of the time. In contrast, fathers convicted of killing their children were sentenced to prison or executed 72 percent of the time and only hospitalized 14 percent of the time. Dahlia Lithwick, a writer for Slate.com, reported on the imbalance in the justice system when it comes to mental health and conviction:

> *The problem with the "illness" theory is that it only goes partway toward explaining why women kill their babies. Illness may explain how some women eventually snap and behave violently. But it doesn't begin to explain why they direct this madness so disproportionately toward their own offspring. Even taking into account that some small fraction of the mental illnesses associated with maternal filicide— most notably postpartum depression—are triggered by the births themselves, the illness theory doesn't explain why mothers suffering from other mental illnesses, or who aren't ill at all, act out with their own children rather than strangers.*
>
> *The illness theory doesn't explain why we don't consider fathers who kill their children to be sick. Pulling murderous mothers out of the field of ordinary criminology and viewing them as fundamentally different raises more questions than it answers. Perhaps murderous mothers are no crazier than fathers. Perhaps murderous fathers are even crazier than mothers. Either way, the failure to view these crimes as morally or legally equivalent reflects a more central legal truth: We still view children as the mother's property. Since destroying one's own property is considered crazy while destroying someone else's property is criminal, women who murder their own children are sent to hospitals, whereas their husbands are criminals, who go to jail or the electric chair.*

> *Why does the legal system treat a mother who kills someone else's child as though she were a sociopathic killer while showing mercy toward a mom who drowns her own? For the same reason the law treats individuals who burn down other people's houses as criminals and institutionalizes those who burn down their own. Men are disproportionately jailed for filicide not because they are more evil than women but because we believe they have harmed a woman's property—as opposed to their own.*[30]

Considering the above, it's no surprise that, mid-trial of the Casey Anthony case, the defense team requested a psychological evaluation to determine if Casey was capable of contributing to her own defense, meaning they wanted to determine if she fully understood the charges against her and was competent enough to proceed. The official motion submitted read, "Based on privileged communications between Casey Marie Anthony and her counsel, counsel reasonably believes that Ms. Anthony is not competent to aid and assist in her own defense and is incompetent to proceed. As a result of this well-founded concern, counsel requests a full competency determination before the continuation of trial proceedings."[31]

A request of competency is not the same as a psychological evaluation to determine whether or not Casey was insane, but for a jury it still raises similar questions. Dr. Kenneth J. Ryan, a criminologist at California State University, differentiates the two by saying, "Insanity, a legal concept more than a concept in psychology, suggests that the defendant has no grasp of what is real and what is not and has no concept of right or wrong. Competency only applies narrowly to the defendant's ability to be a participant in the trial and not merely be the object of the trial."[32] When defendants are deemed "not guilty by reason of insanity," they are essentially acquitted. Even though they did commit the crime they are charged with, such as with Andrea Yates, they aren't held legally responsible for their actions because they weren't aware of what they were doing at the time. Since insanity began playing a role in cases more than two centuries ago, the meaning of the term has altered and expanded, making room for defendants and their attorneys to maneuver psychology to their advantage.

At the defense's request, Judge Perry ordered the competency tests. Three different psychologists—Dr. Harry A. McClaren, Dr. Daniel Tressler, and Dr. Ryan C.W. Hall—examined Casey at the Orange County Jail. All found her competent to stand trial, and the case proceeded two days later. The specific findings from the psychologists were never released.

While a motion to determine sanity was never officially submitted in Casey's case, the competency check certainly ruffled the feathers of the jury. A seed was planted, which allowed the jury to question Casey's decision making process and mental stability. All of a sudden, Casey had an excuse.

The Abuse Excuse

As individuals and as a nation, we all too often make excuses for bad behavior. In the case of Casey Anthony, it's no different. Social media and the broadcast news programs made it possible to learn about the case on an in-depth, personal level, creating a public discourse. Could it be possible, people asked, that Casey is a wrongly accused mom? Is there something in her own experience that can excuse her actions?

Aside from the question of competency, when defense attorney Jose Baez opened the door to doubt and accused George of molesting Casey when she was eight years old, the playing field changed. Casey instantly became a victim, and George's testimony—once a key piece for the prosecution—was no longer seen as 100 percent credible. It was a classic case of the abuse excuse.

Historically, criminal defendants use past abuse (often sexual in nature) as a pity tool to redirect the jury's attention away from the real issue at hand to a side issue that, while horrible, should not affect the outcome of the trial whatsoever. But sadly, what should have an impact and what does have an impact are often very different. Often, sexually traumatized defendants obtain lighter sentences or, in more drastic cases, even acquittals. Often, sexually traumatized defendants obtain lighter sentences or, in more drastic cases, even acquittals. For example, a young man, only sixteen years old, killed his neighbor, hitting him over the head with a ten-pound pickle jar three times and then stabbing him fifty-five times. Although his sentence is voluntary manslaughter and aggravated assault, the young man was only sentenced to five years house arrest.

Criminal defense attorney, Michael Dowd, writes:

> The "abuse excuse" has become a catchy phase describing a decline in moral values marked by circumstances where otherwise guilty people use past victimization to seek absolution for their crimes. The Menendez brothers, Lorena Bobbitt, abused women who slay their abusers and then hide behind the murky 'battered woman's defense', kids who kill because they saw too much violence on television, adults who lash out because of childhood injustices, and women whose acts may be the product of things like PMS and post-partum depression, all leap to mind as examples of a decaying society unwilling to demand individual accountability for criminal acts.[33]

A few days after the verdict came in finding Casey not guilty of all the major charges, I ran into former Los Angeles homicide detective Mark Fuhrman. During the O.J. Simpson trial, Fuhrman was seen on televisions around the world as he testified as one of the lead detectives. He is now a contributor for Fox News and has been an on-air consultant for ABC, CBS, and Court TV.

Within the first few days of discovering their granddaughter was missing, Cindy and George were referred to Furhman, and he flew to Florida to act as a consultant. When I saw Furhman, I immediately asked him the question that millions of Americans were struggling with and continue to struggle with today: "How likely is it that twelve jurors, in a matter of a little more than ten hours, would deliver a clean sweep of a 'not guilty' verdict for all counts of murder, neglect, and aggravated child abuse?"

Furhman replied, "Plain and simple: the jury lacked courage." No one wants to be responsible for finding a young, attractive woman guilty of first-degree murder. "The jury was a bunch of cowards because, if they had convicted her of first-degree murder, they would then have to face the decision of recommending the death penalty."

"The jury didn't want blood on their hands?" I asked.

"I just think they were scared."

Simply put, women killers—by virtue of being the ones who bear children—have a tremendous edge in the U. S. court system, as it operates with an antiquated perception of women, the attractiveness of the women, and the deeply ingrained gender-based excuses that will lessen their punishment. The first line of defense for a woman is either that she is suffering from a form of mental illness or that she suffered through a troubled childhood that has not yet led to a diagnosis of mental illness or insanity, but most certainly will. A suggestion of childhood sexual abuse of a woman defendant can be enough to bias the average individual juror, even in what is supposed to be an unbiased group of people. The term "molested" carries one of the heaviest weights of all words.

Child sexual abuse is still discussed behind closed doors, so if a public accusation is made, no matter what is disproved, the label on the person accused will stick. You can try picking it off like a label on a gift, but no matter how you tear at it, the traces of the price tag are forever etched onto the person.

It was no different with Casey. Once Baez said, "It all began when Casey was eight years old and her father came into her room and began to touch her inappropriately and it escalated. . . She could be 14 years old, have [had] her father's penis in her mouth, and go to school and play with the other kids as if nothing [had] happened,"[34] the tone of the courtroom immediately shifted. Whether true or not, Baez had stirred the pot of confusion and moral outrage in the nation.

As you can imagine, the mere accusation of molestation played out beautifully for the defense. When Casey claimed that her father molested her and brother tried to, it left an indelible impression in the minds of the jury. It didn't matter that there was no evidence to support the molestation charges; George was immediately marked as a questionable character and Casey someone to sympathize with.

Several days after the trial closed, a couple of jurors came forward to express how they came to the not guilty verdict. One juror stated, "We couldn't forget the defense's opening argument that George had molested Casey."[35]

After the case, Mark Lippman, the attorney for George and Cindy, said, "My clients, George Anthony and Lee Anthony, never molested her... And George Anthony had nothing to do with moving the body. And the rest of the things the defense said about my clients in particular never happened... This case has destroyed everyone's reputation. Even if it's baseless, there are people out there that are going to believe . . . for their rest of their lives . . . what the defense told them."[36]

Casey's Motivations

When we peel away the excuses, the lies, and the clutter and confusion produced by Casey and her defense team, we have to ask an important question: Did Casey have the motivation to kill her daughter? What could have propelled her to such extreme actions?

As we've discussed in previous chapters, there are a number of reasons filicide occurs, and Casey, not surprisingly, can claim plenty of those motivations of her own.

1. *Love.* At the time Caylee went missing and was shortly after found dead, Casey was spending all of her time—including nights—with her boyfriend, Tony Lazzaro. She spent countless hours on the phone talking to him and texting him. The two were clearly infatuated with one another.

   Love or infatuation can ultimately be a motivation for murder in unsecure relationships where one person in the relationship wants a child and the other doesn't. Is there the possibility that Tony told Casey he didn't want Caylee staying at his apartment? And when he did spend time with Caylee, did he demonstrate to Casey that her daughter wasn't welcome? During the thirty-one days that Caylee was missing, Casey spent the majority of time at Tony's apartment. Did Tony wonder where Caylee was? Did he bother to ask?

   Inevitably, it's possible Casey wanted to get rid of Caylee so she could continue to please Tony and develop a more lasting relationship. In many ways, she could have seen Caylee as an obstacle for having the type of relationship with a man that she'd always wanted.

2. *Finances.* There is no argument that children are financial responsibilities. Constantly growing, they require food, clothes, supervision, and a roof over their heads. Caylee, of course, was no different, and these necessities for Caylee meant Casey needed a job, something she was plenty happy without. Casey wasn't one for responsibility. She wanted someone to take care of her. And she wanted the freedom to indulge in her own desires rather than her responsibilities.

At the time Caylee went missing, Casey and Caylee still lived at home with her parents, a situation that was taking a turn for the worse. Back in 2006, Cindy and George briefly separated and George moved out of the home. This was ideal or Casey, as Cindy constantly sought Casey's approval, which gave Casey free roam to lead the lifestyle she wanted—shopping, drugs, drinking, and the like. But after a few months absence, George moved home and Casey was no longer able to have a free ride from her mom.

Moreover, with Caylee around, her parents were far more attentive to her finances. Caylee's presence would also keep her parent's always one-step behind her, trying to make sure she was financially responsible in taking care of herself and her child.

3. *Lifestyle.* It can be no surprise that Casey didn't want to live with her parents forever. But the financial, logistical, and emotional responsibilities of being a mother stifled her options.

Whether Tony realized it or not, Casey's ultimate intention was to move in with him. He worked hard running a nightclub, was well known, and led the kind of lifestyle Casey dreamed about. Tony was on his way to a successful career in the entertainment industry, and Casey believed he was her ticket to financial and emotional security. With Tony in the picture, she no longer had to pay money for her partying lifestyle. She was the head guy's girlfriend and that meant free access to get in, to drink, and to act out. In her mind, this also gave her prestige among her peers because he chose her out of all the other girls he came across in the club, and she had no intention of giving that up for a little thing called responsibility.

According to Ashton of the prosecution, Casey's pattern of lying was used primarily to manipulate her mother so she could indulge more in the lifestyle she wanted. For instance, Casey pretended she got a promotion at Universal that required to her be out at night; this would give her the excuse to go out and party. Casey would leave Caylee with her mother, who was willing to baby-sit. When Casey began dating Tony, her reasons to deceive her family expanded. As Ashton described, "He has this life. He's free. He's a club promoter. He's out at night with the loud music ... [with] young people doing what they want to do ... nothing wrong with that. But it's not the life Casey has, because Casey is a mom." Inferring why this would have led Casey to get ride of

Caylee, Ashton continued, "The only way Casey's lies work is if Caylee isn't talking," said Ashton. "Now she's almost … three, and she's starting to become verbal, starting to talk. She can't cooperate [with the imaginary lifestyle] … because she doesn't know enough to lie. At some point, she is going to say something to someone."[37]

4. *Power.* Casey's narcissism was the atom bomb, the nuclear explosion that would break her family's heart forever. When she was growing up, Casey was used to being the center of attention. She was able to manipulate her parents— particularly her mother—into whatever she needed and wanted. When Caylee came into the picture, Casey was no longer the center of everyone's attention to the degree that she was used to. Caylee had become Cindy's primary concern, and Casey couldn't tolerate the shift in her mother's attention.

Unable to financially provide for herself and for her daughter, Casey was dependent upon Cindy and George. But Casey didn't want her parents to raise her daughter. In the same way that she wanted to be the focus of her parents' attention, she also wanted to be the focus of Caylee's attention and affections. Her ego simply couldn't tolerate sharing.

To Casey, Caylee was an object that she possessed, a tool in her toolbox to manipulate those around her—particularly her parents.

Just prior to Caylee's death, Casey had a blowout fight with her mother. Cindy had spent years covering up Casey's behavior to family and friends. Like so many mothers and fathers, Cindy hoped and prayed Casey would one day become the loving and responsible daughter, mother, and woman she had the potential to be. And Cindy hoped that by protecting Casey, Casey would one day realize how much she loved her. But on June 16, 2008, Cindy had had enough. Casey finally took Cindy to a place she never wanted to go: She held Casey responsible for stealing and lying, and she considered calling child protective services and filing for custodial custody of Caylee.

Cindy had been passive to her daughter's behavior for too long. For Casey, her greatest weapon of retaliation was Caylee.

Love, money, lifestyle, and power could all have been influential reasons for Casey to want to get rid of Caylee—a difficult pill for many of us to swallow. We like to believe that women, Casey included, put motherhood above everything. That self-sacrifice comes naturally and constantly. After all, if a mother is capable of killing her own child, then what can we believe in? Where will our emotional security come from if we believe that mothers don't automatically deeply and unselfishly love their children? If we cannot trust our mother's capacity to love us unconditionally as our first and primary caretaker, then life as we know it in the "human race" is left to the dogs with man's inhumanity to man as the dominating behavior. We are left forever asking: if our mother did not love us, then who will?

Conversely, it's much easier for us to believe men are capable of the most heinous crime—killing in cold blood. While we look at men as protectors from the violence of outsiders, we also look at them as creators of violence from within the home. Dahlia Litwick was right on cue with her assessment. Our perception of and exceptions for the genders differ because we believe children are a woman's possession.

But what we forget—and what society has taught us to forget—is that women are human first, women second, and mothers third.

And these tiers apply to Casey, as well. No matter what we might like to believe and hope for—love, money, lifestyle, and power could have plenty to drive Casey over the edge.

The Court of Public Opinion

While Casey Anthony was deemed not guilty by the court system, she reigned guilty in the court of public opinion.

On *48 Hours*, Pam Bondi, Florida's attorney general, said, "No one else could have done this," a strong endorsement from a leading public figure.

When it comes down to it, the biggest threat to Casey was Casey herself. She painted herself as a guilty party, continually deceiving and lying—unlikely actions of a concerned, caring mother. In the early days of her daughter's disappearance, she told detectives, "You can't break me." Not exactly the words of an innocent woman. While the defense peppered photos of Casey and Caylee, they contradicted the truth of Casey's character and the lack of maternal attachment traditional to a mother-child relationship.

The Orange County Sheriff's search warrant, written and signed by Detective Yuri Melich on August 5, 2011, which originated due to "unlawfully commit the offense(s) of child neglect, obstruction of an investigation and false official statements," said: "It should be noted that at no time during any of the above interviews did the defendant show any obvious emotion as to the loss of her child. She did not cry or give any indication that she was legitimately worried about her child's safety. She remained stoic and monotone during a majority of our contacts."[38]

We don't know how Caylee died. Murder? Accident? Natural causes? The investigators don't know; the attorneys don't know; and the autopsy was inconclusive. By the time Caylee was found, it was months after her disappearance, and her remains had decomposed and been ravaged so thoroughly that they told very few stories.

Without hard evidence, the prosecution focused on Casey's flawed character. They explained how she was far more interested in her partying lifestyle than she was in being a mother. She lied compulsively about the case and her daughter's disappearance. And amazingly, when Caylee's remains were found and identified, she hardly seemed affected by the fact that her daughter was dead. But even though Casey's actions are repulsive and nearly impossible to understand, at the end of the day, being a contemptible human being isn't enough to convict, so she was acquitted. When the not guilty verdict came out, public loathing was at an all time high. What people saw—and continue to see—is the significance of the lies Casey told, how she delayed the case, and her total lack of emotion, remorse, guilt, or grief over the disappearance and death of her daughter. The defense came out on the other hand, rubbing it in on how the talking heads had got it all wrong.

"I hope that this is a lesson to those of you who have indulged in media assassination for three years—bias and prejudice and incompetent talking heads saying what would be,"[39] said defense attorney Cheney Mason.

Jose Baez, lead defense attorney, said, "This was a horrible tragedy, an accident that snowballed out of control. The jury saw that and they're the ones that heard all of the evidence, not the propaganda and the speculation and the Frankenstein-like lynch mob that ensued throughout the last three years."[40]

But their word spouting did little to persuade the public.

The term "Dexter Morgan" started trending on Twitter—referring to the show *Dexter* on Showtime, which is about a serial killer who murders individuals who have escaped justice. "Her life could be in danger," said Karin Moore, a law professor at Florida A&M University. "A lot of people wanted to push the needle in themselves, from reading some of the comments made by people online." Vince Carter, an NBA player for the Orlando Magic, said on his Twitter feed, "Casey might want to move out of Florida like ASAP!!"

On July 11, 2011, a *USA Today*/Gallup poll reported that only 1 percent of the public following this landmark trial was convinced that Casey Anthony was a wrongly accused mom. Moreover, at a news conference in Tallahassee, Florida, corrections spokeswoman Gretl Plessinger, referred to the "challenging" number of death threats from the public, as a result of the prevailing belief that Casey was a cold-blooded killer. Plessinger was of the opinion that, "Casey Anthony is one of the most hated woman in America."[41]

What makes Casey Anthony's case such a large cry for justice is that, for the first time, regardless of the excuses offered for such a horrendous crime, or even the cover-up of an "accident" left unreported for thirty-one days, Casey's total lack of remorse, grief, loss, and guilt is so blatant that the public cannot find any redeeming qualities about her.

Jennifer Ford, a thirty-two year old nursing student from St. Petersburg College, was juror number three. After the trial was over and some time had subsided, she finally talked. "I did not say she was innocent. I just said there was not enough evidence. If you cannot prove what the crime was, you cannot determine what the punishment should be... I toggled on manslaughter and not guilty...

It doesn't feel good. It was a horrible decision to have to make. Everyone wonders why we didn't speak to the media right away. It was because we were sick to our stomach to get that verdict. We were crying, and not just the women. It was emotional and we weren't ready. We wanted to do it with integrity and not contribute to the sensationalism of the trial."[42]

In the interview, Jennifer went on to say, "If there was a dead child in that trunk, does that prove how she died? No idea, still no idea... If you're going to charge someone with murder, don't you have to know how they killed someone or why they might have killed someone, or have something where, when, why, how? Those are important questions. They were not answered."[43] And while Jennifer believed Casey was a pathological liar, she noted, "bad behavior is not enough to prove a crime" and a lot of her actions could stem from the family dynamic. "The family she comes from and the family that made her what she is had some influence," she said. "What do they say? You're as sick as your secrets?"[44]

Chapter Four
Emotional DNA

While there are still many questions that linger around the Casey Anthony trial, and while the acquittal no doubt shocked the country, there was one thing no one seemed confused about: the dysfunction of the Anthony family. No one in the courtroom, in the mainstream media, or elsewhere could make the case that Cindy and George Anthony were unfortunate bystanders, simply unlucky to have such a terrible situation fall in their laps. Their actions and words were too tarnished to make such leniency possible. The Anthony family has a long-standing pattern of unhealthy, enabling behavior, and this dysfunction is just another puzzle piece we can add to the larger picture of Caylee's tragic death.

The Pattern of Deception
Often, it's hard to believe the worst in those we're closest to. Instead of trusting in the facts and in common sense, we trust in our hearts and hopes. We make excuses for those we love and care about that we would never make for strangers. *Surely that's not the case*, we say, and then we proceed to list off explanation after explanation for why something could have occurred.

In many ways, this is the trap George and Cindy Anthony fell into, only on a far more extreme level. They hid from the truth, excusing, forgiving, enabling, and denying to the point that Casey was responsible to no one.

Dr. Nancy Darling, formerly of Penn State University, held an in-depth study on why kids lie. The study determined that, at a young age, kids lie frequently and often as a way of avoiding punishment. Dr. Victoria Talwar, an assistant professor at Montreal's McGill University, adds that while we might consider truthfulness to be a paramount virtue, at a young age "lying is related to intelligence . . . It's a developmental milestone."[45]

New York Magazine profiled the study, noting that, "By the time a child reaches school age, the reasons for lying become more complex. Avoiding punishment is still a primary catalyst for lying, but lying also becomes a way to increase a child's power and sense of control—by manipulating friends with teasing, by bragging to assert status, and by learning he can fool his parents. Thrown into elementary school, many kids begin lying to their peers as a coping mechanism, as a way to vent frustration or get attention. Any sudden spate of lying, or dramatic increase in lying, is a danger sign: Something has changed in that child's life, in a way that troubles him."[46]

Talwar adds, "Lying is a symptom—often of a bigger problem behavior. It's a strategy to keep themselves afloat."[47]

New York Magazine continued, "In longitudinal studies, a majority of 6-year-olds who frequently lie have it socialized out of them by age 7. But if lying has become a successful strategy for handling difficult social situations, a child will stick with it. About half of all kids do—and if they're still lying a lot at 7, then it seems likely to continue for the rest of childhood. They're hooked."[48]

But the most disconcerting reason children gravitate toward deception is because they're repeating an activity they've seen practiced in their home, by their role models. "We don't explicitly tell them to lie, but they see us do it . . . They see us boast and lie to smooth social relationships."[49]

"Encouraged to tell so many white lies and hearing so many others," *New York Magazine* writes, "Children gradually get comfortable with being disingenuous. Insincerity becomes, literally, a daily occurrence. They learn that honesty only creates conflict, and dishonesty is an easy way to avoid conflict. And while they don't confuse white-lie situations with lying to cover their misdeeds, they bring this emotional groundwork from one circumstance to the other. It becomes easier, psychologically, to lie to a parent."[50]

In many ways, lies give children some form of stability, particularly in homes where parents are lax on discipline and provide little constancy. Children can lie for the simple reason that they don't know or trust how their parents will handle the truth. They do not feel safe and are begging for structure. Even though children would never admit it or fully realize it, structure and discipline equates to love. It means parents are paying attention, are ready to respond, and that children are secure and wanted.

Darling extended her study into teenagers, looking specifically at how parental discipline affected children's honesty and their relationship with their parents.

"Many parents today believe the best way to get teens to disclose is to be more permissive and not set rules," Darling says. They believe that by letting their child have free reign, they will trust them more and be more open. But the opposite is rather the truth. "Kids who go wild and get in trouble mostly have parents who don't set rules or standards. Their parents are loving and accepting no matter what the kids do. But the kids take the lack of rules as a sign their parents don't care—that their parent doesn't really want this job of being the parent . . . Ironically, the type of parents who are actually most consistent in enforcing rules are the same parents who are most warm and have the most conversations with their kids."[51]

When we look at Darling's and Talwar's research in relationship to Casey and her parents, it's easy to understood how Casey's pattern of deception emerged, grew, and embedded as a constant in her personality. Her parents provided her with no discipline or structure, and her mother, Cindy, provided a prime template to model her deceiving ways after. Put simply, Casey was fertile ground for dishonest behavior.

What is equally troubling, however, and what adds a new dimension, is Casey's lack of regard for how her actions and deceptions affect others. While numerous people are emotionally hurt and while her daughter pays the ultimate sacrifice, Casey doesn't demonstrate grief, loss, guilt, remorse, or regret. This, compiled with her lack of regard for right and wrong, signify something stronger than a simple penchant for untruth. It makes Casey a prime candidate for sociopathic personality disorder.

The Mayo Clinic defines a sociopath in the following context: "Antisocial personality disorder is a type of chronic mental illness in which a person's ways of thinking, perceiving situations and relating to others are abnormal—and destructive. People with antisocial personality disorder typically have no regard for right and wrong. They may often violate the law and the rights of others, landing in frequent trouble or conflict. They may lie, behave violently, and have drug and alcohol problems. And people with antisocial personality disorder may not be able to fulfill responsibilities to family, work or school. Antisocial personality disorder is sometimes known as sociopathic personality disorder. A sociopath is a particularly severe form of antisocial personality disorder."[52]

While I would certainly need to sit down with Casey one-on-one to adequately diagnose her, the cues are all there. The extent and detail of her lack of conscience over the years is profound and markedly disturbing.

So one has to ask: how in the world could her parents—people who saw her every day—not realize it? How could they let behavior, so blatantly troubling, continue?

Like Mother, Like Daughter

Jesse Grund can give insight into the Anthony family in a way many can't. When Casey was only nineteen years old, Jesse fell in love with her and proposed. The two were engaged for a brief period, and he was falsely led to believe, for a time, that he was Caylee's father. Because of his relationship with Casey, Jesse witnessed the dynamics of the Anthony family on a very personal level. "They are not a cohesive, loving group," he told the *Today* show. "That family was a carnival of dysfunctionality . . . (With) Cindy's example of lying, as I've always said, the apple doesn't fall too far from the tree. Casey had to learn her behavior from somewhere."[53]

Almost anyone who has met Casey easily identifies her narcissistic tendencies and propensity to lie. Tracy Conroy, an employee of bounty hunter Leonard Padilla, spent nine days and nights with the Anthony family in 2008, and she described Casey as living in a "completely narcissistic world . . . It was always all about her . . . and when she spoke of Caylee she talked about her in the past tense. It was clear to me she knew her daughter was already dead and [the search for Caylee] was all a big game to her."

"She's crazy, always exaggerating," Tracy continued. "She didn't have a babysitter, she had a nanny. The smell in her car wasn't from one dead squirrel but two. She didn't graduate from high school but she told people she was working on not one but two degrees. It wasn't just her father who molested her but also her brother. She's not of this world. She's a sick woman."[54]

So why is it, when outsiders can so easily identify it, that Casey's own mother, Cindy, misses all the signs? How could she let Casey be so irresponsible? How could she not care enough to know where her granddaughter was? How could she be so in the dark when the truth was looking her so squarely in the face? Surely any woman with a shred of common sense would know that Casey's behavior was disastrous and had the potential to be incredibly destructive.

When boiled down, though, Cindy's motives for covering up Casey's deceit, defiance, and aggression are simple: Cindy desperately wanted the fantasy, an American dream family. She wanted a loving, caring daughter; a beautiful granddaughter; and a healthy marriage. Reality, in particular for the Anthonys, was a far cry from that hope. Cindy and George's marriage was highly unstable, just off a separation, and Cindy's relationship with Casey was extremely volatile. If Cindy didn't give into Casey's demands and if she so much as dared to challenge her, Casey would erupt, pushing her mother further away. So in order to preserve her aspirations, Cindy lived in a constant state of denial, continually excusing Casey's behavior in hopes that their agreement would bring them closer. Even Caylee's disappearance and death weren't enough to wake her from her stupor. If anything, they hardened her resolve. During cross-examination, Cindy Anthony testified that her daughter was a "very loving, very caring mother" who had never mistreated Caylee. What world was she living in?

Rick Plesea, Cindy's brother, frequently traded heated emails with Cindy throughout the investigation and trial. Intense and derogatory though they were, Cindy's brother clearly realized the gaping problems in his sister's logic and her parenting skills:

> *Mom filled me in on Casey so don't lie to me about her. She STOLE dad's check and bought a stupid phone at AT&T so don't lie to me about the $354!!!! Mom has the goddamn statement! I know; I re-verified with mom today!!! The sitter IS the whole case! Are you that dumb??? The house could be JOE BLOWS for Christ's sake. Are you that naive??? You really are that stupid. I can't believe it. My sister is a moron. You need help. You are delirious! I WAS trying to help you. Your granddaughter is dead!! There, I said it. Casey has killed her someway either by accident or on purpose. Casey is a narcissist Read up on it . . . I see how Casey is so screwed up between you and George as role models. Saying Casey will be mother of the year I nearly tossed my groceries. She will be mutha' of the year. Those people in prison will have a field day with her. You better tell her to confess and ask for solitary. It is her only hope. Do you think I care anymore after you attacked me? You are in another universe. You and George ARE on your own. Good luck with that.*[55]

From a psychological perspective, Cindy's consistent and rapid response to excuse Casey as responsible for the death of her granddaughter—accident or murder—is beyond issues of abandonment and enabling. It represents the fragility of Cindy's ego and self-esteem, pointing toward Dependent Personality Disorder. *DSM-IV* defines Dependent Personality Disorder as a pervasive and excessive need to be taken care of that leads to submissive, clingy behavior and an intense fear of separation. Traditionally, it begins by early adulthood and is identified by five or more of the following symptoms:

- Needs an excessive amount of advice and reassurance from others in order to make decisions.
- Needs others to assume responsibility for most major areas of his or her life.
- Difficulty expressing disagreement with others because of fear of loss of support or approval. Does not include realistic fears of retribution (i.e. vengeance or justice).
- Has difficulty initiating projects or doing things on his or her own (because of a lack of self-confidence in judgment or abilities rather than a lack of motivation or energy).
- Goes to excessive lengths to obtain nurturance and support from others, to the point of volunteering to do things that are unpleasant.
- Feels uncomfortable or helpless when alone because of exaggerated fears of being unable to care for himself or herself.
- Urgently seeks another relationship as a source of care and support when a close relationship ends.
- Unrealistically preoccupied with fears of being left to take care of himself or herself.

Cindy's utter dependence and need for Casey was unhealthy. But just how severe was her need for love and approval? Could it have caused her to willfully participate in Caylee's death or, at the least, its cover-up? Throughout the trial, there were specific times Cindy's truthfulness was questioned and many wondered if she would face perjury charges due to allegations she made on the stand.

The Questionable Internet Searches

Cindy testified that she personally made Internet searches on her home computer during the afternoons of March 17 and March 21, 2008. She said she was searching for chlorophyll because her dogs were getting sick from bamboo in the backyard. She mentioned she also searched hand sanitizer because someone had told her that it was unsafe to have around children. However, time card records from her work, Gentiva, indicated that she was at work at the time and couldn't have made the searches herself.

Gentiva's chief compliance officer, John Camperlengo, testified and presented records that showed Cindy's account was logged in on her office computer from 8:02 am until 6:00 pm on March 17. The records showed that someone was entering patient data using her account during the time around 1:40 pm when the chloroform searches were being done at the house. He also showed records from March 21 indicating that Cindy logged in at work from 8:43 am to 5:37 pm, with active data entries at the time of the relevant searches that day, too.

Moreover, Deborah Polisano, Cindy's supervisor at Gentiva, testified that it was very unlikely Cindy left the office for multiple hours in the middle of the day. Polisano also noted that office computers would turn off after a short period of inactivity, so no one else would have been using Cindy's login.

The prosecution asked forensic experts to examine the computer, and Sgt. Kevin Stenger testified that he examined all deleted Internet history files from March of 2008 and did not find anything relevant to chlorophyll, hand sanitizer, or bamboo. Stenger also indicated that the term "neck breaking" had been typed into Google. And Detective Sandra Osborne testified that she searched the Anthonys' entire hard drive for any of the terms and only found chlorophyll in the dictionary. Bamboo was found often, but never in relation to anything poisonous.

The Pool Ladder

In a similar matter of inconsistency on the part of Cindy, Detective Yuri Melich testified about Cindy's phone records. Cindy had stated previously that she called George on June 16 or 17 because she came home and found the ladder attached to the pool. Since the defense had made the case that Caylee drowned, this was certainly beneficial to their position. However, there weren't any records that Cindy called George that entire week— either from the house phone or cell phone.

The Unmistakable Stench

One of the most questionable acts, of course, was how Cindy dealt with Casey's car. When George brought Casey's Pontiac Sunfire home, Cindy made a remark how it "smelled like something died in the car." Caylee's favorite doll was in the back seat and had the same remarkable stench. And while to Cindy's credit she did call 9-1-1, she also proceeded to clean the car, as well as Caylee's clothes and doll she found in the backseat, washing away any possible forensic evidence.

We all have things we're willing to do for our children and family members that we wouldn't do for others. But there are moral and legal lines that shouldn't be crossed—no matter who for. In her desperation, Cindy crossed unthinkable boundaries. She overlooked and justified to an extent that ended up being detrimental to her granddaughter. If Cindy had stepped in earlier and disciplined Casey accordingly for her actions, would this situation have occurred? With Casey, as always, very basic acts of accountability were sidestepped and ignored. Who, in the whole mix, was acting like a responsible party? Certainly neither of the mothers.

An Adult?

The Casey Anthony we all saw in the media and on trial was terrifyingly immature and self-serving. In an article in *Psychology Today*, Dr. Jennifer L. Tanner addressed an important question: Was Casey Anthony an adult?

The question, in a way, sounds silly. Legally of course she was. She was a twenty-two year old charged with first-degree murder and tried in an adult court. But her behavioral patterns indicate that she saw herself as anything but.

This question of adulthood coincides with the question of deception. Where did the pattern start? And why was it allowed to continue? Without Cindy and George's assistance, it's not likely that Casey would have been able to ignore her responsibilities as a mother without serious consequences? But tough love wasn't a part of Cindy or George's vocabulary and, as a result, Caylee became the collateral damage.

Like many teenagers who are growing and maturing, Casey wanted the freedom of adulthood without the responsibilities. Casey, as Tanner points out, "dated and had sex with multiple partners. She considered getting married, but she didn't. She didn't have steady work and she didn't have a steady relationship. She lived at home with her parents. She made very little expected progress gaining independence from her parents. She was uncommitted to adulthood."[56]

Cindy and George enabled this behavior. As Casey didn't have an income, they provided food, clothing, and shelter for both Casey and Caylee. Casey used Cindy's car. Many of Casey's friends, as Tanner points out, referred to Casey as a "fun and loving mom." They reported that Casey was always "happy." But was she a responsible mom? No one asked that question. When spending time with her friends, did Casey ask her friends to be quiet while Caylee was napping? Did Casey's friends see Casey buying milk and diapers for the baby? I would have liked to have heard responses to questions such as: did you ever hear Casey talk about her visions for a future with Caylee, the things she wanted to give to Caylee, the type of home she wanted to provide for Caylee?"[57]

The truth is, as Tanner so eloquently puts, "We don't know how involved Casey was in parenting Caylee before Caylee went missing. What we didn't hear about in this case is what happened at night when Caylee was overtired. What happened when Caylee had a stuffy nose and couldn't sleep at night? When the day grew long and it was dinner-time and then bath-time and then bed-time, when that same routine was demanded for days and then weeks and then years, who was taking care of that routine every day and every night? What happened when it wasn't play-time? What happened when it was responsibility time? In the end, when Caylee needed an 'adult,' who was there?"[58]

The Passive Party

"The complaint among my friends," one middle class housewife told me, "is trying to structure the kids' time. It's a constant struggle getting them to do their homework, eat their dinner, shower, go to bed on time, etc. etc. It seems like I'm always saying 'do this' or 'do that.' And then, when I'm already feeling like the bad copy, my husband comes swooping in, just in time for playtime. 'Daddy can I have this?' they say. 'Daddy can I have that?'—hoping he'll give them a better answer than mean old mom did."

This woman, of course, is not alone. Many mothers report how thoroughly exhausted they are serving as the primary caretakers. And while these are often very valid concerns, we often miss the other side of the coin. Some mothers become so controlling and co-dependent on their children, that the father becomes disenfranchised. Instinctively, these mothers become so overprotective of the child, that no matter what the dad does, he's going to fail.

Despite the length of their marriage, George and Cindy had a clearly volatile relationship, in which Cindy, for all intents and purposes, wore the pants. As a result, I have no doubt George must have endured a significant amount of frustration as a husband and as a father, living with a manipulative, lying daughter like Casey, who was indulged by her mother's dependent personality.

"Controlling people are very insecure people and encourage passive aggressive behavior in the people around them because they will tolerate no truth that disagrees with their point of view or any challenge to their authority," writes Evelyn Leite, an author, counselor, and trainer recognized for her efforts in family systems, mental health, addictions, and grief therapy. Ms. Leite goes on to say, "In the relationship arena one will often see women who are very much in charge of everything and usually they have in tow a man who appears to be gentle and easy-going. Often the man goes out of his way not to incur her wrath. Because she will put him down and embarrass him for not being the aggressive creature she thinks could meet her needs."[59]

George instinctively knew something was wrong long before Caylee went missing. However, he consistently gave in and abided by Cindy's chaotic rants, verbal abuse, and deception, playing the role of the coward. One of the key instances of George's acquiescence is when he went to take lunch to Casey at the sporting goods store where she said she worked, only to find out from the manager that she wasn't employed there. When George told Cindy, she erupted. But not for the reasons you'd think. Instead of being mad at Casey for lying, she was mad at George for prying into Casey's life, afraid that their tampering would push Casey and Caylee away. Rather than standing up to Cindy and holding their daughter accountable, George gave in, chalking it up to agree to disagree in the many differences between them.

This same response would repeat itself when it came to Caylee's disappearance. During Casey's first release from prison on bail, George grabbed Casey and held her up against the wall yelling, "Tell me what you did with her. Is she dead? Is she alive? Where is she?"

True to pattern, Cindy interceded and swooped Casey upstairs, happily helping her clean up and relax. While Casey was home, she didn't participate in the search for Caylee, nor did she exhibit any grief or loss. George commented later that her emotional state didn't appropriately line up with that of a woman who had just lost her daughter. But rather than try to get Casey to confess, he put his true feelings aside and remained passive. As Rick, Cindy's brother, wrote in an email, "If I had five minutes with Casey I would beat the information out of her. Her stupid parents need to kick the crap out of her and find out the real truth. Enough is enough…. She is so guilty it is ridiculous. Five minutes is all I ask."[60]

Throughout the years, particularly early on, George had a strained relationship with his family and never fully wanted to be around them. In later years, as an almost apologetic maneuver to display his loyalty, George became very dependent upon Cindy, condescending to her every request. Cindy, however, was very aggressive and hostile toward George, alienating him as a parental figure. People who knew the Anthonys well often heard Cindy refer to him as "stupid" or told him to "shut up" in front of the kids. In a way, his passive response was almost him agreeing to take punishment for his prior mistakes.

What's interesting about this is that George's passive behavior is very contrary to most men in his prior, but long-served profession. Male police officers tend to dominate by maintaining emotional control and boundaries with their wives and children. Many officers choose submissive wives, allowing them to be the man of the house. But George, despite his prior career, simply does not fit the bill of a homicide detective in his own home. He had, and I assume continues to have, tremendous difficulty knowing how to cope with his wife's high anxiety and her constant need to pretend. Like so many men, he tried to keep a peaceful home. Unfortunately, his need to be liked by both his wife and children crippled his ability to be an effective parent. By acting as a pacifist, he wasn't able to instill the characteristics his daughter needed to become a functioning member of the family and of society.

George is now a man shouldered with deep regret, and he is less two of the closest members of his family: his daughter and his granddaughter. From the moment Caylee was identified and pronounced dead, everything he had been suppressing came up to the surface and the guilt of his actions—or, more telling, his inactions—became nearly unbearable. In her book, *On Grief and Grieving,* Elisabeth Kübler-Ross writes that the first stage of grief is loss and denial. For George, Caylee was his hope in life, and the idea that his daughter, Casey—the child he raised—could have murdered his granddaughter, and thereby his hope for the future, was simply too much to bear. In his helplessness, on January 22, 2009, George Anthony attempted suicide. A transcription of the hand-written note was logged in the court records at the time of the trial. A few significant excerpts are presented:

- I blame myself for her being gone. You know for months, as a matter of fact, for a year or so I brought stuff up, only to be told not to be negative;
- Caylee Marie—I miss her. I want my family back;
- Going back to why I cannot live anymore, I cannot function knowing our granddaughter is gone. Caylee Marie never had a chance to grow. I wanted to walk her to school (The 1st day). I wanted to help her in so many ways. Shoot her 1st basket. I could go on;
- I sit here empty inside for her;
- Caylee, here I come.

George admits he repeatedly asked himself how he missed the warning signs and what he could have done differently. The answers, no doubt, generated a tremendous amount of guilt. The thing about George, which is so significant, is that he knew better. He didn't deny and lie to himself. Instead, he suppressed the truth. And he felt that by his passivity, he hadn't protected Caylee—the one person who was still pure and genuine in his life.

As easy as it would be for us to consider George as just a poor, maligned scapegoat, he is no victim. He chose his behavior just as much as Cindy and Casey chose theirs. While the public begs Cindy to wake up, George's submissiveness, while quiet, is equally troubling and worthy of blame. While the two aren't guilty of murder, their faults at parenting opened the door for things to spin wildly out of control. And so spin they did.

Bad Blood

When Casey was released from prison on July 15, 2011, she didn't go home. George Anthony made it clear that his daughter wasn't welcome. It is, of course, little surprise that George didn't run to his daughter and comfort her in the aftermath of such a tumultuous period. If they didn't foster enough animosity prior to the trial, the case certainly dissolved the links of familial bond.

Despite his passive behavior as a member of the Anthony family, George was a lightning rod in the courtroom. Throughout the trial, he was accused of a number of cringe-inducing acts, including molesting Casey when she only a young child; having an affair with a woman during the search for his missing granddaughter; and participating in Caylee's death and cover up.

The molestation, which we discussed prior, was a homerun for the defense. Without having to provide a shred of evidence, they were able to cast doubt on George's credibility, tainting the jury's perception of a key witness. The other hot button issue, which provided similar effect, was George's alleged affair with Crystal Holloway (aka River Cruz), which occurred during the search for Caylee. George met River in 2008 at a command center the Anthony had set up in partnership with Equusearch, an organization that helps find missing people. George said he considered her a friend and that he visited her house two or three times, all with Cindy's knowledge. "The very first time, I was in there because we had a conversation in which she relayed to me probably weeks or just a few days prior...that she has a brain tumor, she was dying, she needed someone to comfort her.... I felt that she was so giving of herself, to me and my family, to help look for our grand-daughter, it was the least I could do to go in and show some compassion and respect."[61]

Despite River's accusations that the two had been intimate, George firmly denied them, saying that he needed many of those people in his life at the time, and that he had nothing to hide.

Research shows that it's very common for someone to lean on the opposite sex during a time of crisis or death, imminent death, or murder. Even if it's the loss of someone who has been expected to pass from a long-term cancer or HIV, it's not unusual for spouses to split apart for a moment and later come together. Some separate permanently because the crisis is too much for the relationship to withstand. However, couples that weather the storm find that the event becomes deeply personal to their relationship dynamic and history together.

But despite research and, yet again, a lack of evidence, the defense had done their job well. The public's scathing response was nothing short of puritanical judgment. How could a husband be unfaithful to his wife in such a terrible time? People cried. What kind of person is he? The distraction was near perfection and people failed to discern what they should have. Even if he did commit this alleged dalliance, while not applaudable, it in no way is evidence of any wrongdoing as it relates to Casey or Caylee. Whether or not George had an affair has nothing to do with whether he was guilty or not in Caylee's disappearance and death. It was a sideshow to distract from the case's greater truths. And to the detriment of justice, it was effective.

Nevertheless, this alleged affair, along with the molestation accusations, greatly affected the way George was viewed. The foreman of the jury said everyone had doubts about George Anthony's character and involvement in Caylee's death. Juror number 11, said George acted like he had "selected memory" and "... that, in itself, was something that I always kept in the back of my mind for every time that he got up there. I was just kind of on guard for that.... With the can, the selective memory, the way he handled the tow yard incident, River Cruz, the lady he could have had an extramarital affair with, it raised questions. It really did."[62]

The Grand Disconnect

Now that the defense has pled its case, the verdict is in, and Casey is a free woman, there is even more division in the house of Anthony. In their first major media appearance since the trial, the married pair went on Dr. Phil to come clean once and for all. And while speculations of Caylee's death have been rampant since the jury said the final word, none have, perhaps, been as intriguing or narrow-minded as those from Caylee's own grandparents.

Even though the two haven't talked since the trial, it's not surprising that Cindy still defends her daughter. She believes there's merit in the defense's storyline of drowning, telling Dr. Phil, "I buy the part that Caylee drowned, but I don't buy the circumstances surrounding the drowning . . . I believe that justice for Caylee was when her mother walked. I believe that with all my heart because I know the love that those two had and I know that Caylee's soul would never have rested . . . I believe it was an accident and until someone can prove differently that is what I believe."[63]

As an excuse, Cindy even suggested that Casey was prone to seizures which made her unable to clearly discern what she was doing—an excuse, Dr. Phil says, is nothing more than Cindy Anthony refusing to accept reality.

"I don't know why she's having a seizure. Does she have a brain tumor? Were the seizures caused by stress? I don't know what happened, and that's what I want to find out down the road."[64]

But the seizures Cindy refers to don't cause unpredictable behavior and a propensity to lie. Dr. Enrique Serrano at the University of Miami School of Medicine told NBC News, "If the patient is fully recovered after a seizure, there shouldn't be any changes in their personality or behavior."[65]

George, however, was on the opposite end of the spectrum from Cindy, and this time he wasn't mincing words or suppressing. "I believe something else happened to her... I believe Casey or someone else she was with possibly gave too much to Caylee. She fell asleep and didn't wake up." By 'too much,' he was referring to "possibly some kind of drug or something like that." George believes Casey would have drugged Caylee up so she could "go out and have a good time. To be with friends."[66]

Cindy looked like her world had shifted. "This is the first time that I've heard this out of his mouth. I'm really kind of shocked to hear that today."[67]

"I don't want to see my daughter put to death, but I wanted her held responsible for my granddaughter. I did, and I still do," George continued.

Now the outspoken member of the family against Casey, George signed a growing, online petition for Caylee's Law—a law that would make it a felony for a parent or guardian not to notify law enforcement of a child who has gone missing within twenty-four hours, a clear dig at his daughter's actions.

"Caylee's Law will be groundbreaking," he said, "and will be up there assisting the Adam Walsh Act, the Lungsford Act, Amber Alert, and many others that are necessary for our children."

Cindy, however, did not such thing, even admitting that while she understood how it would be difficult for George to accept her in the house again due to Casey's accusations, she would like to be reunited with her daughter. "I would love to see her be happy either in a career or in a family setting. You know, I'd love for her to get married if she so chooses and, if she's healthy, to be a mom again."

"It's denial of the highest order," Dr. Phil said. "It's like, 'I'm going to find some reason to say this was involuntary on (Casey's) part, whatever it is she did.'"[68]

No Room For Excuses

If I were treating Casey and interviewing both her and her family, I'd be looking for a number of things. What is her history as a child and adolescent? I would want to know about her schooling, friendships, and her relationship with her brother. Were there incidents of trouble at school? Did she have any mental health issues that needed to be addressed by a professional or school counselor? What was her dating history? Etc.

Likewise, I'd want to do a full Mental Status Exam (MSE) on George and Cindy, observing them individually and asking in-depth questions as to personal issues, family, psychological, financial, medical, and relationship history.

I would also want to interview them together to observe their body language, communication, and similarities and differences in their understanding and perception of their relationship. For example, I would be interested to know when George and Cindy got together, what was their relationship like and what drew them together? These are all key items to know because it sets up the dynamics of them from the beginning. How you start a thing, after all, is how you finish it.

No one outside of the Anthony bubble will ever know the full story. It's too convoluted and complex to simplify into a black and white answer. What we do know, though, is that the Anthony family is a tangled web composed of a number of characters who made poor choices. Cindy and George could have done a better job. They could have provided Casey with a more disciplined lifestyle that engrained in her a sense of responsibility and a strong moral compass. And how they raised Casey did have a significant impact on how she performed as a mother.

But as Carl Pickhardt, a psychologist from Austin, Texas, wrote in *Psychology Today*:

> *It is hard for parents to be by love attached to their grown child and not become unhappily emotionally entangled in the process, disappointment and guilt among the chief emotional offenders. What is required at the end of their child's adolescence is the hardest act of parenting there is - letting be and letting go. But that is what they have to do to free up all concerned.*
>
> *At the beginning of childhood a stranger is born dependent on parental care. At the end of adolescence a more independent young person departs their support. In between these two events, a loving connection has been established that hopefully will sustain and nourish the parent/adult child relationship through the years ahead. A healthy intergenerational connection requires having an adequate separation of responsibility that recognizes the psychological independence between them.*
>
> *Subscribing to this separation, parents can honestly say and mean this. 'Our grown children are not meant to be ourselves, to repeat ourselves, to reflect ourselves, to affirm ourselves, to complete ourselves, to repay ourselves, to absolve ourselves, or to fulfill ourselves. They are simply meant to be themselves. And our job is to respect their right to independent choice and value the individuals they have turned out to be.'[69]*

When considering Casey's potential role in Caylee's death—whether it be murder or accident—it's easy to turn and point the finger at Cindy and George. The environment Casey was raised in enabled her behaviors and fostered a personality prone to selfishness and deceit.

Because of how they raised her, one could argue, Casey was able and willing to commit these terrible acts. But what does pointing fingers and passing blame accomplish? And at what point does a parent have to let go and a "child" have to take responsibility?

Considering my past experiences and current profession, I have a strong belief in excuse free living. Past circumstances can certainly influence present behavior and even can make it more understandable, but no matter the emotional or physical scars you've suffered, you still have the ability to make your own decisions and live an upstanding life. The defense team tried admirably to point the finger somewhere else—anywhere else. From Zanny the Nanny, to George, to Cindy, everyone was culpable for the crime except for Casey herself.

But as Dr. Tanner from Rutgers University explains:

Arguing that 'her childhood made her do it' may work as a legal strategy, but it doesn't work as a psychological explanation for her behavior. Ms. Anthony's defense attorney claims that learning to keep the secret of being molested trained her to keep secret the drowning of her daughter. However, with respect to the scientific literature, childhood experiences do not translate into adult behavior in a 1:1 correspondence. That is: not everyone who has a bad childhood exhibits bad behavior in adulthood and not everyone who had a good enough childhood exhibits good behavior in adulthood. Drawing connections between childhood trauma and adult outcomes when connections were faint at best got Freud into a lot of hot water. (Think Baez can do better?)[70]

Tanner goes onto argue that rather than the idea that it was childhood that made her do it, the answer could be quite the opposite: perhaps it was her adulthood. Casey was acting like the majority of kids her age. She was partying. She was trying different things out, dating multiple people. She was exploring the options for what she wanted in life. But the only problem was that Casey wasn't normal. She was a twenty-two year old girl with a two-year-old kid. She had missed the exploratory stage and had gone straight into adulthood—a period in life where the opportunity to be selfish and narcissistic is no longer there. When you have a child, your focus immediately goes to your baby; it's a necessity.

Our preconceived notions of motherhood don't want to believe that something as simple as selfishness could drive a woman to get rid of her child. Instead, we'd rather have a scapegoat. We'd rather point at Cindy and George and make them responsible for Casey's actions. That's simply easier to swallow. And, let's be honest, that made that rather easy. But no matter how frustrating, confusing, and irresponsible Cindy and George's actions are and were, they were not the ones who were truly responsible for Caylee's death. Jesse, Casey's former fiancé, said in an interview, "What would I say if I saw her today? I would tell her she needs to repent, because at the end of the day, she is going to have to answer for why Caylee isn't on this earth anymore."[71]

And it's true. Everyone has his or her reasons to act out. Everyone has the difficulties of the past or present. But everyone also has the ability to make his or her own choices. And everyone—including Casey—will have to answer for what those are.

Chapter Five
Red Flags, Telltale Signs, and Hindsights

It was the morning of June 20, 2001 that Rusty Yates' phone rang. It was his wife, Andrea, who he had just left at home about an hour earlier.

"You need to come home," she said. She was calm and composed. Non-plussed.

"What's going on?" he asked.

"It's time. I did it . . . it's the children."

His heart dropped.

"Which one?" he asked.

"All of them."

Andrea Yates, then thirty-seven years old, drowned all of her children in the bathtub: her six-month old, Mary; two-year old, Luke; three-year old, Paul; five-year old, John; and seven-year old, Noah. She killed them one by one then laid them in the bed beside each other face up to rest.

Then, just as calmly, she called to confess.

"Who killed your children?"

"I killed my children."

"Why did you kill your children?"

"Because I'm a bad mother."

By the end of the day, she was charged with capital murder for "intentionally and knowingly" killing three of her children. She was not charged for the murder of her two youngest sons.

From the beginning, the defense made a plea for not guilty by reason of insanity. Throughout the initial trial, the defense called several expert witnesses. And while they varied on the specific diagnosis, they all agreed that Andrea was psychotic at the time she killed her children. She believed she failed them as a mother and, therefore, had to relieve them of their lives.

Time magazine reported:

> *After her arrest, jail psychiatrist Melissa Ferguson testified, Andrea was put on medications that enabled her to finally talk about the visions and voices that she says guided her actions. It was only after she was placed in a jail cell, naked, on suicide watch that Andrea spoke of the Satan inside her and the only was to be rid of him: She had to be executed. And she had to kill the children, as Satan demanded, to get the death penalty. Andrea tried to explain. 'It was the seventh deadly sin. My children weren't righteous. They stumbled because I was evil. The way I was raising them they could never be saved,' she told the jail psychiatrist. 'They were doomed to perish in the fires of hell.'[72]*

But the first jury didn't bite. In March 2002, a Texas jury found Andrea guilty of capital murder. They sentenced her to life in prison with eligibility of parole in forty years. However, in 2006, due to faulty testimony from Dr. Park Dietz in the first trial, a Texas Court of appeals reversed the convictions and Andrea was given a new trial. After only three days of deliberations, she was found not guilty by reason of insanity and committed to North Texas State Hospital.

The not-guilty verdict in the Andrea Yates case—as with so many others—was extremely controversial. People are wary it's a cop out, an easy means of avoiding life in prison or, worse, the death penalty. But the prosecution argued that Andrea deserved the lenience. She suffered from postpartum psychosis, her attorneys argued, and it was this mental illness which forced her into a delusional state where she believed she was saving her children from Satan. "She needs help," the jury foreman from the 2006 trial said at a post-verdict press briefing. "Although she's being treated, I think she's worse than she was before. I think she'll probably need treatment for the rest for her life."[73] The defense called the verdict a "watershed event in the treatment of mental illness."

But the prosecutors didn't agree. They believed Andrea failed to meet the specific requirement of insanity as detailed by Texas law. More specifically, she failed to have a severe mental illness that prevented her from distinguishing right from wrong. In Texas, the law on insanity sets the bar high. While Andrea had been hospitalized four times for psychiatric care, had attempted suicide twice, and while there were thousands of medical documents demonstrating her psychosis, the prosecution believed Andrea was still able to understand right from wrong and that her murderous actions were intentional and executed, not insane.

The difficulty in the Andrea Yates trial, as well as so many other murder trials, is distinguishing truth from falsehood. The jury had to discern if the defense was looking for the convenient out, making her actions coldblooded, or if she truly had the signs and symptoms of a woman manipulated by mental illness. And in order to intelligently make this call, it was essential that the twelve men and women hear her personal history, as well as expert analysis.

Prior to becoming a wife and mother, Andrea was a successful student, graduating high school as valedictorian of her class, an officer of the National Honor Society, and captain of her swim team. She would go on to become a nurse at the University of Texas, M.D. Anderson Center where she thrived. It seemed like she was an on an excellent path. However, when Andrea married Rusty and began a family, her mental health began to deteriorate. While she seemed to cope with the births of her first three children, after the birth of her fourth child she became depressed.

In June of 1999, the spiral started. Andrea attempted suicide by overdosing on pills and was hospitalized as a result. While in care, she was prescribed medication by her first psychiatrist, Dr. Starbranch, and was told not to have any other children due to the mental complications that could evolve. However, when Andrea was released from the hospital, she discontinued the medication. Her symptoms became worse and worse, and she began to engage in self-mutilation, where she cut herself. She stopped feeding her children because, in her delusional state, she believed her children were overweight. Her paranoia became so acute that she believed there were video cameras in the ceilings of her home and that the television was talking to her. Inevitably, she threatened suicide again and her husband, Rusty, found her with a knife to her neck. Andrea begged Rusty to let her die stating, "The children are not developing well." She was hospitalized again where she remained in a catatonic state for ten days. During this hospitalization, doctors put her on the anti-psychotic drug, Haldol, and she responded well. Andrea and her husband agreed she had returned to her old self with the medication and she was released.

However, this state of mental clarity would not last long. Although Andrea and Rusty had been warned she must not stop taking the Haldol or have another child, with Rusty's encouragement, Andrea stopped the medication and became pregnant. Another hospitalization ensued and Andrea began treatment with a different psychiatrist. For reasons that can only be attributed to a lack of thoroughness, the psychiatrist, Dr. Mohammed Saeed, discontinued the Haldol, believing Andrea was no longer psychotic, and released her from the hospital after ten days. Dr. Saeed told her "to think good thoughts." Only two days after her last appointment, she murdered her five children.

Andrea's story is tragic, not only because of the loss of her children, but also because of how those around her did not take her postpartum psychotic episodes seriously. She had delusions, obsessive thoughts, and hallucinations. She was suicidal and vocal about her inadequacies. However, when told of her hallucinations, her husband did nothing to monitor her symptoms or change the care of their children temporarily so that Andrea could work on recovery. If anything, Rusty encouraged her deterioration, not taking her psychotic episodes seriously. Her psychiatrist, Dr. Saeed, did likewise. And as a result, five innocent children had to pay.

The Andrea Yates story is a prime example of how we, as a society, process the unthinkable act of filicide. When we associate mothers with murder, our minds automatically flash to mental illness. Because of our preconceived notions about who mothers are and how they're supposed to behave, we believe there has to be emotional and intellectual instability for a woman to do something so horrific as to harm or kill her child. But Andrea is not unique. Over two hundred women kill their children per year, and that's just ballparking it. The actual figure is probably much higher. "I'd say a mother kills a child in this country once every three days, and that's a low estimate,"[74] says Cheryl Meyer, co-author of *Mothers Who Kill*

Their Children. And many cases likely go unreported or unnoticed, particularly among mothers with newborns and those who hide their pregnancies.

So why is this important, you want to know? Why do we have to focus on something so horrifying and repulsive? Isn't it just easier if we pretend this isn't happening? If we chock it up to people with a few lost marbles and not a prevalent problem in our society?

Well, easier, yes. Proactive, no. The problem with ignorance and disregard is that they both are prime breeding grounds for problem proliferation. When we pretend we don't see the signs like Andrea's husband and doctor did, we allow a situation that could be contained to spiral out of control. Indeed, it's our very reluctance to acknowledge a mother's capacity to kill, which makes our ability to prevent further occurrences—through understanding and reacting to the telltale signs—nearly impossible.

"We've learned how to reduce auto fatalities among kids, through seatbelt use. We've learned how to stop kids from strangling on the strings of their hoodies. But with this phenomenon, we struggle," says Jill Korbin, an anthropologist at Case Western Reserve University who has studied mothers who kill children. "The solution is not so readily apparent."[75]

Part of the problem is the perpetrators aren't always so easy to identify. There's not a specific "type" of woman who kills. It spans race, income, and upbringing. Appearance and age. We can't profile with any kind of convenience or accuracy. But despite these differences in background and types, there is a common denominator among mother murderers: their reasoning. Meyer and her co-author, Michelle Oberman, found in their studies that there are five key reasons mothers murder:

- Filicide related to an ignored pregnancy: murder of an unwanted newborn
- Abuse-related: murder as a result of physical abuse
- Neglect-related: murder as a result of neglecting a child, such as malnutrition
- Assisted or coerced filicide: murder which is assisted or forced by another human being, such as a husband or partner
- Purposeful filicide: the intentional murder of a child

What's interesting about these five reasons is that the majority necessitate a mental illness or personality disorder in the mother, providing common ground for identification. Yes, of course, not every mother who has been diagnosed or who displays symptoms of a mental illness or personality disorder is at risk of killing her children. But these are tipping points that can lead to tragic thinking and actions. As filicide is so hard to combat, the more we can identify and prevent, the more children we'll have in safe homes.

When I was listening to the news and participating in the media circuit throughout the Casey Anthony trial, there is no surprise that the issue of mental illness was tossed liberally around the media, if not directly in the courtroom. Did Casey suffer from mental illness? What could have caused her actions? Was she delusional? Did she hallucinate? Was she another Andrea Yates? Surely, she couldn't have killed sweet Caylee in cold blood. And yet with all the gabbing, it amazed me how many terms were thrown around—often incorrectly—about the psychological reasons she could have taken her daughter's life. Mental illness isn't guesswork—it's a science. And a misdiagnosis is just as bad as no diagnosis.

As we evaluate Casey and try to understand her motives, its essential we key in on the reasons women kill—as listed by Meyer and Oberman above—while also clearing the air and providing easy ways to understand the key psychological terms necessary for identification and diagnosis. By starting from a more complete foundation of knowledge, we can better recognize and comprehend the actions of Casey Anthony and those like her—as well as prevent others from committing similar tragic actions in the future.

Identification

There are generally two types of mothers who murder their children—those diagnosed with mental illness or those diagnosed with a personality disorder, also referred to as character-logical disorder.

For many people, mental illness is a difficult thing to grasp; there is a stigma surrounding it and a large barrier when it comes to understanding, diagnosing, and treating the various forms it takes. According to Janine Robb, Executive Director of Health and Wellness at the University of Toronto, "Mental health problems and illnesses can affect anyone at any age . . . People have a hard time understanding things that they can't see and understanding information that is not felt to be relevant. Due to inaccuracies and misunderstandings, people have been led to believe that an individual with a mental illness has a weak character or is inevitably dangerous. People are often fearful and rejecting of people with mental health problems."[76]

However, despite people's reticence when it comes to the topic, according to a report from the Surgeon General, "during a 1-year period, 22 to 23 percent of the U.S. adult population—or 44 million people—have diagnosable mental disorders."[77]

Mental illnesses, according to the National Alliance on Mental Illness, are medical conditions that disrupt a person's thinking, feeling, mood, ability to relate to others, and daily functioning. While there are a number of mental illnesses, the primary ones found in mothers who murder are postpartum depression, postpartum psychosis, and major depressions, such as severe and recurrent.

Many people I've talked to who are uneasy about the idea of mental disorders have a hard time coming to terms with their reality because mental disorders don't tend to have physical symptoms like a broken bone or cancer. In other words, if we can't see it, how do we know it's real? How do we know someone isn't just temperamental, sad, or in the mood to be alone?

To this end, when we discuss psychological disorders, the first thing we have to clearly understand is what a disorder is. How specifically can we establish what is abnormal versus what simply might be considered odd or off base?

"Being 'odd' could mean that their behavior or thinking is rare; out of the *statistical norm*," says Juan Salinas of the University of Texas, who clearly explains:

> But what about people who have high intelligence or are artistically gifted? Those traits aren't statistically frequent but we wouldn't call smart or artistic people abnormal. Being 'odd' could also mean that a person's behavior isn't meeting certain social norms of the people around them. But those standards can vary between cultures (in some cultures, for instance, burping at the dinner table after eating is considered a compliment to the cook) and even within our own culture standards can vary between social groups (the behavioral excesses that might tolerated from a guitarist in a rock band would likely be unacceptable from an bank teller).

So views of suitable social behavior aren't absolute. Some cognitive or perceptual distortions, such as hallucinations clearly are abnormal. But what about milder distortions or perceptions of reality like inflated egos or unusually high self-esteem? Some might say that feelings of personal distress like depression or anxiety are abnormal. But such feelings might be reasonable under some circumstances such as the death of a loved one or the loss of a job. Only one trait seems to be clearly important in all cases, and that is behavioral maladaptiveness. A clear sign of abnormal behavior or mental state is when an individual's behavior is destructive to themselves or their social group, such as family, friends or co-workers. More than any other sign harming the welfare of one's self or those close to one's self is most universally accepted as indicating an abnormal mental or behavioral state.[78]

Once we have a clear understanding of what disorder is versus what normal behavior is, we can more easily identify mental illnesses and personality disorders.

Legal Defense

As the Andrea Yates trial showed us, mental illnesses have come to play a key role in our court system. When an attorney wants to pursue the possibility of mental illness in his or her client, the defense team will normally start by making a motion stating that they do not feel their client is "fit to stand trial" or "cannot assist in her own defense." After a review of independent court-ordered psychological evaluations, the judge makes the final determination if the defendant is "competent" or "incompetent" to stand trial. If the defendant is found "incompetent" to stand trial, the trial may be continued, but the defendant will be placed in a state mental hospital until deemed competent or until he or she is convicted as guilty and sentenced to a state mental hospital. If competent, the defense attorney may enter a plea of "not guilty by reason of insanity." If the psychological evidence causes the jury to come to the conclusion that the defendant was "insane" by the legal standards of the particular state at the time the crime was committed, then the sentence is usually served in a locked mental health hospital until the defendant is well enough to be reintegrated into society.

As you can imagine, the insanity defense is a source of incessant dispute among those in the legal field, as well as those in the public. There is an overwhelming belief that defense teams are exploiting the plea to evade more significant charges for their clients.

In discussing the insanity defense, Mark Gado of TruTV writes, "One of the cornerstones of the criminal justice system in America is the concept of *mens rea*, a Latin phrase that translates to 'state of mind.' In order for a person to be held criminally liable in the courts, our system demands that that he or she must have criminal intent or awareness of the wrongfulness of the act. If a person is mentally ill and unable to tell the difference between right and wrong, for example, then he or she cannot be held criminally culpable in our society. That principle upholds the dignity of the court and ensures those without malicious intent, such as the mentally retarded, will not be unfairly punished."

Diagnosing

The mental health community utilizes the American Psychiatric Association's *Diagnostic and Statistical Manual of Mental Disorder* (DSM)—in other words, the holy grail of all things psychiatric—to classify mental disorders and provide diagnostic criteria. Within the

DSM, now in its fourth edition, is the use of a multi-axial system that facilitates comprehensive and systematic evaluation. Some people have a dual diagnosis. This means they have both a diagnosis of mental illness, what we refer to as an Axis I diagnosis, as well as a personality disorder, known as an Axis II diagnosis.

A Mental Status Examine (MSE) helps to diagnose a depressive disorder or mood disorder. The MSE is a combination of the observations of the person's state of mind and body language, family history, mental health history, personal biography, social information, and medical history that may be the cause of or have an impact on the individual's diagnosis of a depressive disorder.

Women who are diagnosed with a mental illness who murder their children report having had feelings of depression, powerlessness, resentment, and frustration. They have difficulty expressing and acknowledging their anger about their lives. Unfortunately, the child is the one thing they feel they should be able to control, but the child's place in their life requires a level of responsibility that makes them feel out of control. These women may feel a momentary sense of relief or control immediately after murdering their child, until inevitably they realize what they have done.

On the other hand, some women continue to believe afterward that they were good mothers, doing the 'right thing' for their child. These women suffer from what I refer to as the "good mom syndrome." They believe that by killing their children, they are doing what is best for them.

Unthinkable? No.

Who in their right mind would think such a thing? However, what's even more shocking is how often it's said. Consider Andrea Yates, who believed she was a bad mother and was saving her children from Satan. And she isn't alone. Numerous other women who kill their children believe they're acting in the best interests of their sons and daughters. Lita Linzer Schwartz, who is a professor emeritus of psychology and women's studies at Penn State, said, "We see cases where the mother thinks the child would be better off in heaven than on this miserable earth. They think it's a good deed, a blessing."[79]

Ms. Oberman agrees. "It's how the sick mother sees herself being a good mother. Once she decides she can't bear the pain anymore, she thinks, 'what would a good mother do?'"[80]

In Korbin's studies, where she conducts in-depth interviews with prisoners, she finds the same results. "Often the people around these women will minimize a troubling instance that they see, saying, 'Well, she's a good mother.' We err on the side of being supportive of women as being good mothers, where we should be taking seriously any instance where a mother OR father seems to be having trouble parenting. ANY instance of child maltreatment is serious."

Mental Illness

So let's dig deeper. Within women who murder due to mental illness, there are typically three culprits: postpartum depression, postpartum psychosis, and major depression.

Major Depressive Disorder

According the National Alliance on Mental Illness, "Major depression is a serious medical illness affecting 15 million American adults, or approximately 5-8 percent of the adult population in a given year. Unlike normal emotional experiences of sadness, loss or passing mood states, major depression is persistent and can significantly interfere with an individual's thoughts, behavior, mood, activity and physical health. Major depression disorder ranges from mild to severe, single episode or recurrent, and with or without psychotic features, catatonic features, and/or melancholic features. A cluster of these features, leading to major depression, also known as clinical depression, can have a disabling affect on all areas of an individual's life, causing significant distress and a lack of control over his/herself, circumstances, and environment. According to the DSM "five (or more) of the symptoms have been present during the same 2-week period" and "at least one of the symptoms is either (1) depressed mood or (2) loss of interest or pleasure."

Signs and Symptoms of Major Depression

1. Depressed Mood: Feelings of hopelessness, emptiness, loneliness, sadness, tearful, irritable, social withdrawal

2. Anhedonia: Loss of pleasure and interest in daily activities; decreased sex drive

3. Disturbances Sleeping: Insomnia or hyperinsomnia, a.k.a. oversleeping

4. Weight: Altered appetite with a 5 percent change in weight within a month's span

5. Fatigue: Low energy or exhaustion

6. Psychomotor Agitation or Impairment: Impaired speech and writing

7. Worthlessness: Feels guilty all the time, like he/she is not enough, low self-esteem, even self hatred, helplessness, difficulty in relationships

8. Lack of concentration: Short-term memory issues, indecisive, has difficulty thinking and focusing

9. Suicidal Ideation: Thinks about committing suicide daily, may have a plan, or has made an attempt

Postpartum Depression

Like major depression, postpartum depression is a serious mental illness. However, this depression is a direct result of expecting and having a child. Up to 15 percent of women suffer from it.

For years, postpartum depression was thought to be hormonal, but now has taken a new direction. Within recent years, the diagnosis and understanding of postpartum depression has become far more prevalent in society. Previously, people believed women were just experiencing an extended bout of baby blues. However, the baby blues only last a few weeks—postpartum depression is far more severe; the onset can begin in prenatal pregnancy or post-child birth and can last through the first year of a child's life.

Women who have reported these symptoms may have pre-existing signs of a mental disorder or distress triggered prenatally or with the birth of their child, such as: generalized anxiety with panic attacks, depression, and bipolar disorder. Studies on pre- and post-pregnant women reveal there is no correlation between postpartum depression and hormonal changes.

Signs and Symptoms Unique to Postpartum Depression

1. History of Depression, Bipolar Disorder, Panic Attacks: Predisposed to a recurrent mental illness; symptoms return such as a manic episode; crying spells

2. Newborn has health problems: The baby is temperamental or colicky

3. Guilt: They are not happy with or about the baby and feel totally disconnected to maternal instincts

4. Social Withdrawal: Reluctant to tell others, which leads to isolating themselves; they have little social support or help

5. Failure: The mother is unable to bond with the newborn, feels like she can't take care of the baby and can't stand the sight or the sound of the baby
6. Inability to Breastfeed: Emotionally, the mother must use formula
7. Obsessive Thoughts: The mother feels violent toward the baby; outbursts of anger
8. Anxiety: Panic attacks; sudden or chain cigarette smoking

Postpartum Psychosis

Postpartum psychosis is a rare and extreme form of postpartum depression. Like postpartum depression, it develops generally one month following childbirth. Women who have postpartum psychosis often feel unemotional from their newborns, as well as other people in their life that they are traditionally close to. This disorder includes both depression and at least one psychotic episode. Many women suffer from hallucinations and delusions; display bizarre behavior; and may have the urge to kill herself and her child or children. As the DSM-IV states, "Psychotic features appear to occur in from 1 in 500 to 1 in 1,000 deliveries and may be more common in primiparous women"—otherwise known as women giving birth for the first time. Women who have had post-partum psychosis with their first child have a 30-50 percent chance of a repeat of this diagnosis with the birth of a second child, and so on. Overall, postpartum psychosis is the primary diagnosis for mothers who murder their children.

Signs and Symptoms of Postpartum Psychosis

1. Delusions (The mother believes she is saving the child from the devil, that the devil has possessed the baby, or that the baby has special powers and must be stopped)

2. Obsessive Thoughts (The children are dirty with sin; a mom must be punished for her sins; the children are unhealthy; her sins are now her children's sins)
3. Hallucinations (Hears commands and voices, most often believe God is commanding them. Believes she saw an evil spirit in the child)

PROFILES OF MOTHERS WHO MURDER
Mental Illness

Kenisha Berry

On November 29, 1998, in Jefferson County, Texas, Kenisha Berry bound and gagged her four day old son, wrapping duct tape across his body and mouth and stuffing him in a black plastic trash bag, finally leaving his body in a dumpster. Convicted in February 2004 of killing her baby, the Texas Court of Criminal Appeals in May overturned her death sentence and remanded her to prison with a life sentence because prosecutors failed to establish in that she presented a future danger to society. She will be forced to serve at least forty years before being eligible for parole.

In 2007, Berry was charged with wrapping her baby daughter, Parris, in a pillowcase, and throwing her in a ditch abandoning her in 2003. Berry gave birth to both of her children at home, alone, four and a half years apart. According to court documents, she kept all the pregnancies a secret. Testimony at trial reported that Berry (like Casey) could not hold down a job responsibly. After dropping out of high school, Berry earned a General Equivalency Degree (GED) and became a prison guard. However, her job only lasted four months; she was fired due to her continual tardiness and absences. More than that, at the time of Berry's arrest for throwing away Parris, Berry worked at a day care center babysitting other babies and children. Motives for Berry's behavior: power, dominance, and lifestyle.

Dena Schlosser

In 2004, shortly after the birth of her third child, Schlosser was diagnosed with postpartum psychosis. Concern for her child prompted an investigation by the

Texas Child Protective Services in which they reported that she was not a risk to any of her children's safety. By the end of the same year in a psychotic episode, Schlosser believed that God commanded her to murder her eleven-month-old baby by severing his arms and allowing him to bleed to death. Schlosser also believed that God told her to cut off her arms as well. She was found "not guilty" by reason of '*insanity*.'

Schlosser and Andrea Yates were roommates in the same Texas psychiatric hospital. Schlosser now walks free on these conditions: never get pregnant again and must take a "physician-approved birth control prescription"; all visits with her ex-husband and two surviving daughters must be supervised; attend outpatient psychotherapy once a week; take all psychotropic medications prescribed, and see her psychiatrist weekly.

Michelle Kehoe

In December 2009, Michelle Kehoe was convicted of the first-degree murder of her two-year-old, Seth Kehoe, and attempted murder and child endangerment of her seven-year-old son, Sean. Kehoe wrapped duct tape over Sean's mouth while he struggled watching her "hurting his little brother." She then turned for Sean and began slashing his throat and neck. She had already finished murdering little Seth by slashes to his throat.

Kehoe admitted to the premeditated murder of her two sons months prior to her fatal attack on them. She believed she was saving them from suffering from the major depression she felt was destroying her own life. Kehoe went on to admit that she purchased the knife with the intention of murdering her sons. Kehoe's defense of claiming 'insanity' was based on a long history of major depression and suicide attempts; however they were discounted. It did not appear from the evidence that she had the intention of killing herself along with the children.

The Kehoe case is a tragic one, not only for her sons and their father, but for her as well. Kehoe was a victim of sexual molestation by her "step-father, nephew, and neighbor." It was reported that Kehoe suffered for years with severe, recurrent major depressive episodes. It was disclosed in court documents that she had attempted suicide at least three times that were known of, including one with her children in the car by driving into the Iowa River at a freezing temperature. Kehoe had mental health hospitalizations, tried anti-depressants and forty-four electroshock therapy treatments; however, nothing worked. Her children should never have been allowed to remain in her custody.

Shannon Steibach

On May 20, 2008, a neighbor found Shannon Elizabeth Steinbach, a thirty-three-year-old mother from Denison, Iowa, hanging in the basement of the house, along with the lifeless body of her four-month-old daughter, Hope, who was located in approximately five to six inches of water in the bathtub upstairs. It was ruled an apparent murder-suicide. Those who knew her had no idea there was a problem. Clearly, nobody knew her that well.

Although we will never know for sure why Shannon killed her daughter, her behavior was consistent with someone suffering from severe postpartum depression. There must have been signs of a problem, but nobody saw them.

Personality Disorder

Anti-Social Personality Disorder

According to the *DSM*, personality disorders represent "an enduring pattern of inner experience and behavior that deviates markedly from the expectations of the culture of the individual who exhibits it." Generally speaking, these patterns tend to be steady across a variety of circumstances, and while the individual might believe he/she is acting in a fitting manner, these "appropriate" actions can be harmful to the individual and to others around him/her.

Within personality disorders, anti-Social Personality Disorder (APD) is the primary diagnosis of mothers who murder their children. However, in the field it's a controversial diagnosis since researchers can't definitively assert the cause and origin. In the 1800s, the very first diagnosis for a sociopath was "moral insanity." By the 1900s, in an effort to narrow down the meaning of "moral insanity," the name changed to "psychopathic personality." The DSM III would change it once more in the 1900s to "anti-social personality disorder, (APD)" and it has remained the same by the DSM-IV in the new millennium.

Currently, the most utilized theory of APD's development is bio-psychosocial—a combination of genetic, environmental, and psychological factors coming together. In other words, nature and nurture working together to produce a result. The predominate factor of the biological and genetic factors is centered in the pre-frontal cortex, temporal lobes, and with the neurotransmitter Serotonin in these specific regions of the brain. All three regulate mood and behavior, particularly impulse control and aggressive behavior seen in APD.

Environmental factors, which play a role in the development of anti-social personality, include parenting in early childhood development, the learning of boundaries, reward and consequences, the learning of coping strategies, school, and the interaction with family and friends. Based on the trials of women who have murdered their children and appear to fit this disorder, the "How?" and "Why?" is much more complicated than their social and family history. As in the trial of Casey Anthony, we cannot simply say, "If it weren't for her parents," or "Cindy made her this way." APD is far more complex.

The *DSM* defines APD as a "lack of regard for the moral or legal standards in the local culture. There is a marked inability to get along with others or abide by societal rules. Individuals with this disorder are sometimes called psychopaths or sociopaths." In order to be diagnosed, an individual must have shown signs of a conduct disorder prior to age fifteen, then, he or she must have shown signs of increased symptomatic behaviors by the age of eighteen.

Signs and Symptoms of Conduct Disorder before the age of 15
- A pervasive pattern of violating the rights of others: Violates societal norms and regulations

- Destruction of property: Fire setting, blowing up, damaging
- Aggression against people and animals: Killing, injuring, threatening or harming
- Deceitfulness and Theft: Pathological lying

Signs and Symptoms of APD at age 18 and Older
- Repeated acts that could lead to arrest
- Conning for pleasure or profit, repeated lying, or the use of aliases
- Failure to plan ahead; being impulsive
- Repeated assaults on others
- Reckless disregard for the safety of themselves or others
- Poor work behavior or failure to honor financial obligations

Common Behaviors from Individuals Diagnosed with APD
- They are often described as easy to talk to, charming, or charismatic;
- They are hostile and domineering;
- They feel powerful when humiliating others;
- They are filled with rage and act vengeful;
- They have a low frustration tolerance and are prone to verbal outbursts;
- They have an inflated sense of self and believe they are always right;
- They believe they have certain powers and abilities;
- They exaggerate reality;
- They feel as though they can talk their way into or out of anything;
- They participate in deceit for personal profit or pleasure;

- They are commonly pathological liars;
- They are manipulative and secretive and are able to justify anything;
- They have an incapacity for emotion;
- They feel contempt for other people's feelings and have no true connection to feelings of sincerity, tears, warmth, love, happiness for others, sympathy or empathy. When they do display an emotion, it serves an ulterior motive. Cold, detached, does not respond within normal range of reactions to something wrong, someone hurt, dead etc.;
- They lack shame, guilt or remorse;
- They are callous and have a total disregard for others feelings;
- They have a constant need for stimulation;
- They live on the edge and are promiscuous and gambling;
- They live for the moment, forgetting the past and not thinking about what consequences their future actions hold;
- They desire immediate rewards and gratifications;
- They become easily bored, needing constant change;
- They are highly impulsive with no sense of personal boundaries;
- They have a history of behavioral issues and academic difficulties, but they "get by" by conning others;
- They have a problem making and keeping friends;
- They are irresponsible and unreliable;
- They don't accept blame even for acts they obviously committed;
- They are constant finger pointers;
- They are sexually promiscuous and commonly participate in infidelity;

- Often child sexual abuse and rape are a portion of their backgrounds;
- They lack a realistic life plan;
- They tend to move around a lot, making constant promises for the future;
- They have a poor work effort but they exploit others effectively.

PROFILES OF MOTHERS WHO MURDER
PERSONALITY DISORDER

Darlie Routier

In 1997, Darlie Routier was found guilty of murdering her two sons, Damon and Devon. During the trial, Texans grew to hate Routier because the prosecution demonstrated her concern for her opulent lifestyle overshadowed her concern for the life of her two boys. She had been living the American dream, which included a house, two cars, a boat, a husband, kids, and no job. But they were living beyond their means. And when her husband had a huge drop in his income, they knew they needed to change their lifestyle; but Routier didn't want to. Instead of stepping down her lifestyle to accommodate their new financial circumstances; her solution was to get rid of the boys.

Much like Casey's partying and celebration with her tattoo "Bella Vita," the picture presented to the jury was someone who showed no tears, bereavement, remorse, or guilt. She was convicted of first-degree murder and sentenced to death.

China Arnold

China Arnold was not new to the prison system when she was convicted of killing her twenty-eight day-old baby girl, Paris. After an argument with her boyfriend over the paternity of Paris, China, out of anger at her boyfriend, walked into the kitchen and cooked her baby in the microwave for two minutes. The effort to introduce evidence of mental illness at the trial was not successful. Arnold only wanted to show her boyfriend who was in control. Out of a sheer need for power and dominance, she cooked her baby from the inside out. Her attitude, "Fuck you. I bet you care now." China was convicted of aggravated murder and is currently serving a life sentence.

Susan Smith

On July 22, 1995, Susan Smith was sentenced to life in prison with no possibility of parole for murdering her two young sons, Michael, three years old, and Alexander, fourteen-months-old. Smith is as close as we come to Casey Anthony. Smith's unconscionable lies, much like those of Casey, forced police and the community to waste valuable resources on an all out "manhunt" for nine days. Smith's actions parallel the way Casey manipulated the media and the public into a false belief that they were searching for suspects who had committed a crime. Smith's husband's grief paralleled that of grieving grandfather, George.

Smith and Casey do differ in one significant way: the issue of sexual molestation. We know there is no evidence of Casey being molested. However, we certainly are aware that the cry of molestation is often used to create empathy for her behavior. There are plenty of copycat liars who use the unfortunate tragic life stories of others in defense of their own profound lack of morals and behavior.

At sixteen years of age, Smith bravely came forward and told both her mother and the Department of Social Services that her stepfather was sexually molesting her. Rather than support her daughter, Smith's mother took the defensive position of being more upset with Smith for making it public than for her husband's sexually abusive behavior. As a result, Smith was ridiculed and left to deal with her stepfather's sexual abuse on her own. As it would turn out, Smith could prove sexual abuse at the hands of her stepfather. Ultimately, he openly admitted to molesting her.

The strange twist came with Smith continued to have consensual sex with her stepfather as an adult. I say strange in that, under most circumstances, reporting abuse to the authorities by the victim is an empowering step toward healing. The victim is then less likely to have consensual sex with the perpetrator as an adult. The term "consensual" can be misleading. It refers to the age of the victim in this case. I say victim because Smith's abuse began as an adolescent, and it is difficult to ascertain the emotional duress or circumstances in which a sexual relationship developed into adulthood. There is simply not enough known about the relationship between her and her stepfather. Despite her mother, this tells me Smith did not receive the emotional help she so badly needed from social services.

These factors of her childhood neglect and emotional abuse by her mother, and having sex with her stepfather as an adult, can help us understand Smith falling along the lines of an Axis II diagnosis of a character-logical disorder. But this in no way excuses the cold blood murders of her little boys; it simply gives us a greater insight into her lack of emotional development. Smith has difficulty in a number of important personal and social development areas, such as: all-or-nothing thinking; unwillingness to take personal responsibility; lack of attachment;

lack of boundaries; narcissism; abandonment issues; and lack of concern for the safety of her children. Nevertheless, there is still no direct correlation between her emotional and mental stability and the fact that she murdered her children. Smith lacks the ability to have emotionally intimate relationships, making her less likely to see how her behavior affects others; she still knows right from wrong. Her intellect is still intact. Her motive for murdering her children was love, money, and lifestyle.

After receiving a letter from her boyfriend, Tom Findlay, that stated, "I think that you are a terrific person. But like I have told you before, there are some things about you that aren't suited for me, and yes, I am speaking about your children," Smith was fearful that her rich boyfriend was going to break up with her because he was not ready for a family. Smith's solution was to get rid of them. So she put her sons in their car seats, claiming she was "suicidal," and was going to her mother's home. Instead, she drove for a while, then went to the local lake, knowing there was a ramp from which the car could accelerate and she could watch as her children drowned. Smith reported to the police that she was a victim of a "carjacking" while her children where in the car.

How Casey Fits the Mold

So what does this tell us about our key player, Casey Anthony? When we evaluate her in light of this knowledge and other cases of mothers who have murdered, it's clear to me that she suffered not from a mental illness, but from a personality disorder. Ever since she came on the public stage, it was evident that she lacked the history of depression, guilt, social withdrawal, and feelings of failure so often associated with mental illness. If anything, she was the opposite. She was carefree, consumed in public life, and nearly joyful.

Casey walked around with the self-understanding that she could talk her way out of anything. She was charismatic and charming, while also being hostile and domineering. She was a pathological liar and manipulated others at will. Her exaggerated perception of self and reality made her believe she could lead the police and public where she liked; and unfortunately, when her not-guilty verdict rang in, she got what she wanted.

Judy Kuriansky, a psychologist from Columbia University, said, "It would be exceptionally difficult for anybody to treat her. There is no magic pill that's a truth serum for a person who's a pathological liar." And for Casey, of course, the question is why would she want to be treated? By the jury's verdict, she was rewarded for her lying and given a free pass. Kuriansky continued, "Why would she want to go to therapy when she basically got what she wanted? There is no motivation for her to seek help. If she had been sent to jail, maybe she would want to see somebody because her style didn't work, but it did.

And unfortunately for Caylee, it always has.

Chapter Six
The Verdict Is In

One of the most phenomenal things about the Casey Anthony trial was hardly the story, the lies, or the deceit, but the complete fascination from the American public, particularly from mothers themselves.

The search for Caylee Marie resonated deeply with the significant percentage of women who have given birth and raised a child. And the obsession was far more than a fixation with maternal murder. Everyone knew it was a case against the unfit mother—it was disappointing, horrifying, but more than any of that: terrifying. The selfishness and indifference displayed by Casey was every mother's deepest, darkest, most terrifying thoughts come to play in real life.

"What we're really fixated on," writes Bonita Burton of the *Orlando Sentinel*, "are the great motherhood taboos on trial. The unimaginable horror of losing a child holds less interest for us than the perfectly imaginable horrors of our deeper subconscious fears. Hard questions are being asked about the unspoken psychic weight borne by all mothers—especially working mothers, especially single working mothers. Is my mother-baby bond bulletproof? Will people think I'm evil if I have a good time away from my children? How much will motherhood decrease my marketability in the singles world? What if my nanny turns out to be a psycho? If I move home with my parents, will my child love them more than me? How much of the monotony and sacrifice of bringing up a baby can I really take—what if I snap and someone, even accidentally, gets hurt? Add the rare public scrutiny of the conflicted feelings many grown daughters have toward their mothers—the frustrated love, and even, sometimes, the hatred—and the trial becomes irresistible . . . Being a mother is supernal joy, but that doesn't mean it's not hard or sometimes even horrible."

The scariest thing about Casey Anthony was that she wasn't an Andrea Yates. She was of sound mind and her sound mind told her to do despicable things. What we hate about Casey Anthony so much, and why the nation continues to be in such an uproar, is that she shows us that women and mothers, people our society so reveres, are capable of committing the most atrocious acts. She verified that women are humans first, women second, and mothers third. And at the end of the day, many of us simply aren't prepared to deal with that.

An Angry Nation

To call it an uproar is to be markedly understated. If you read any of the papers, watched any of the news shows, followed any of the Twitter feeds or Facebook posts, the consensus was in. Per the court of public opinion, the jury was wide of the mark. According to a number of polls taken across the United States, seventy percent of the public believed the jury made the wrong call.

> *Huffington Post*
> - Do you agree with the verdict?
>   Yes: 30.63%
>   No: 69.37%

Cleveland.com

- Do you agree with the verdict?
  Yes: 20.18%
  No: 79.82%

NJ.com

- Do you agree with the Casey Anthony verdict?
  Yes: 18.96%
  No: 81.04%

uppermichiganssource.com

- Do you agree with the verdict in the Casey Anthony trial?
  Yes: 25%
  No: 75%

CBS 6

- Do you agree or disagree with the Casey Anthony jury's verdict?
  Yes: 23%
  No: 77%

Q104 Radio Station

- Did the jury make the right decision?
  Yes: 17.39 %
  No: 82.61 %

KTLA.com

- Do you agree with the jury's not guilty verdict in the Casey Anthony murder trial?
  Yes: 16 %
  No: 78%

Al.com

- Do you agree with the Casey Anthony trial verdict?
  Yes: 23.03%
  No: 76.97%

But while Casey was released with but a minimal slap on the wrist, thanks to public scorn and enmity, her life outside prison doesn't promise to be cake walk pretty. Cheney Mason, one of Casey's attorneys, referred to the public as having a lynch-mob mentality.

"She's gone, she's safe, and elaborate plans had to be made to keep the people away from her," he told NBC's *Today Show.* "Her life is going to be very difficult for a very long time as long as there are so many people of the lynch-mob mentality."

Jose Baez believed the media played a significant role in encouraging public rage. "Pundits and media personalities have no right to try and alter the life of any individual because of what they think may or may not have happened."

Carole Lieberman, a forensic psychiatrist at UCLA, agreed. "The main reason that people are reacting so strongly is that the media convicted Casey before the jury decided on the verdict. The public has been whipped up into this frenzy wanting revenge for this poor little adorable child. And because of the desire for revenge, they've been whipped up into a lynch mob."

Regardless of the reason, the public verdict remains alarmingly strong and vocal. Mark Nejame, a prominent attorney in Orlando, said, "It's obvious she is the most despised person in America. And especially in Florida—and specifically here in Central Florida. People are incensed, and many people have lost all sense of reason. They are very passionate about her acquittal. Her personal well-being is at stake."

Karin Moore, a law professor at Florida A&M University, said, "I suspect she's not going to have a very pleasant life. This will follow her wherever she goes . . . Her life could be in danger. A lot of people wanted to push the need in themselves, from reading some of the comments made by people online."

Casey, always prone to be believe she can lie and charm her way out of anything, initially probably failed to understand it isn't celebrity that surrounds her; it's ill repute. And while the bulbs may flash and the people may fawn, it isn't because they adore her; it's because they're revolted by her, her actions, and her ability to come off *scot free.*

Since being acquitted, the biggest question revolving around Casey is no longer her guilt or innocence, but her ability to have any sort of a life at all. Where will she live? Will anyone hire her? Does she have a family anymore? During the case, she dismantled everyone closest to her—claiming her father and brother molested her as a child and that her mother was a domineering control freak. She has few allies left amidst a country fully equipped with anger. Throughout the trial and after, Anthony's defense team received numerous notes threatening physical or fatal harm to Casey, swearing revenge against her should they ever see her in public.

Gregory Jantz, a psychologist based in Seattle, says Casey's predicament is ripe with problems. "This is a girl who needs help . . . It's a very dysfunctional family system that could explode."[81]

Moving Beyond the Mob Mentality
The most difficult thing to do in a case like this is let it go. Casey seems clearly responsible—in one manner or another—for Caylee's death. And in turn, we want justice. Hard, loud, fair justice.

Casey showed us the worst side of humanity. She put out on public display what mothers truly are capable of. She showed us the dark side, and we resent her deeply for it.

But now that the legal system has run its course and Casey is free, we have to ask ourselves how valuable it is to blow our horns and bellow our threats? Perhaps—despite our hatred for her actions and, therefore, her—and despite our deep desire to see her punished, there is something else we can direct our energies toward that would be more beneficial? There must be a way we can move beyond the lynch mob.

On the Dr. Drew's show that aired on July 11, 2011, he keyed in on the very danger of letting our anger overtake us, "This is dangerous stuff. Somebody is bound to get hurt . . . And the fact is, a mob mentality needs a catharsis. And without a catharsis, the mob continues to swell and circulate. And let's be very cautious with this. Don't contribute to this. I certainly don't want a frenzy because of something we've said here. Let's move on . . . let's funnel our energy in a positive direction. Not just for Casey—not just for, rather, Caylee, but for all of us . . . Resentments are like taking a poison and expecting it to hurt somebody else. You're building up resentments and it's not good for any of us."[82]

We as a society need to come to terms that tragedy and abuse can come from anywhere. Certainly, it can be the result of mental illness and insanity. But it can also come from a woman who does not have a tragic background with a terrible, twisted family dynamic of abuse. Anyone—female/male, mother/father—can make the unimaginable choice to murder one's children. As Hazelwood puts it, "It happens in families where there's no history of violence and where there's a long history of violence. It crosses racial lines, socioeconomic lines. It's not black, Hispanic or white, rich or poor. It's a horror that we as a society are going to be confronted with again and again."[83]

During the Casey Anthony trial, I came to realize time and time again that the excuses we make as a nation for women who kill their children are preventing them from being tried and convicted in a fair and balanced manner. We must free ourselves of the stereotypes and myths that all mothers want their children, love their children, and aren't disappointed at the difficulty and responsibility of raising a child.

I believe it's time as a nation that we pay closer attention to the signs and symptoms of women who, like Casey, prove over-and-over that they are unreliable and negligent as a parent. It's time we stop worrying about stepping on toes and start being a vigilant community, particularly with those who are consider to be our immediate friends and family.

Deanne Tilton Durfee, the executive director of the Los Angeles County Inter-Agency Task Force on Child Abuse and Neglect, said, "When it comes to deaths of infants and small children... at the hands of parents or caretakers, society has responded in a strangely muffled, seemingly disinterested way ... The parents commonly have a history of previous violence, social isolation, substance abuse, and poverty."[84]

Susan Hiatt, the director of the Kempe National Center for the Prevention and Treatment of Child Abuse and Neglect in Denver, explains that "generally parents who kill their children tend to be under a lot of stress. They may be very young and not ready for the demands of parenthood. In all likelihood, they are socially isolated and do not have a large social net. They may have been victims of violence themselves."[85]

In other words: there are signs and symptoms, precursors to the horrible act itself. Whether it be an unfit mother or a mentally-ill mother, there are identifiers along the way that foreshadow trouble.

Consider Casey. She was young; clearly unprepared to be a parent. She wanted to be a socialite and her responsibilities as a mother deprived her of all the opportunities she wanted. She lied continuously, was unable to keep down a job. Constantly she put her welfare above her child's.

Signs for trouble? I would say so.

Suzanne Barnard, a social worker at the American Humane Association, recounted her meeting with a woman who had killed her young child. "She had substance abuse and mental illness problems. Her husband had left them. She felt that she had no future and that the child had no future. I asked if she knew about all the ways she could get help, from public assistance to family members. She had no idea. She had been abused herself. I felt profound sadness and helplessness. Although I had access to community resources, we hadn't connected in time to prevent this tragedy."[86]

Dewey Cornell, a clinical psychologist at the University of Virginia says, "I don't think most parents who murder children wake up in the morning and say, "This is the day I'm going to kill my kids." Usually one thing leads to another, and the problem escalates to the point where eventually the person caves in under the pressure and stress . . . The major message from this is to try to appreciate how important it is to educate people and help them to become better parents."

So the question is: How do we proactively help?

Making a Case for the Unfit Mother

I won't lie; this can get ugly. There seems to be a great deal of gray area when it comes to identifying a truly unfit mother. Anyone who has been a mother knows well that parenting isn't always roses and potpourri. There's frustration, disappointment, and times where nothing is wanted but peace and solitude. And because we know just how difficult mothering is, we hesitate in pointing the finger. We falter in saying what needs to be said: *You're not up to snuff. How you act and care for your child is dangerous.*

But holding your tongue is holding out on the truth: while not all unfit mothers will harm or kill their children, some certainly will. History has proven it. Again and again. Knowing this, you have to ask yourself a very real and very important question: What's more important, not stepping on toes or protecting our children?

Consider it this way: What do you wish Cindy and George Anthony would have done?

When it comes to the legal world, it's often very hard to prove a mother unfit. It is against our very nature to do so, and, as a result, there has to be credible evidence of her neglect and/or incompetency.

In *Family Law: Examples and Explanations*, Dr. Robert Oliphant and Nancy Ver Steegh write, "By the 1920s and 1930s, many American jurisdictions replaced the paternal preference with the 'tender years' maternal presumption. Children of 'tender years' included preschool children and sometimes children through the age of ten. These young children were seen as best cared for by mothers who would provide for their physical and emotional needs while the father was working away from home."[87]

In *Freeland v. Freeland*, the concept of a mother's superior love was highlighted and how our concept of this love taints the justice system: "Mother love is a dominant trait in even the weakest of women, and as a general thing surpasses the paternal affection for the common offspring, and moreover, a child needs a mother's care even more than a father's. For these reasons, courts are loathe to deprive the mother of the custody of her children and will not do so unless it be shown clearly that she is so far an unfit and improper person to be instructed with such custody as to endanger the welfare of the children."[88]

While in present-day time strides have certainly been made to show that a father is just as capable of loving and caring for a child as a mother is, society as a whole, including our court system, still winces at removing a child from the motherly nest unless absolutely necessary. However, sometimes, no matter how much we dislike it, it must be done.

So what to do?

If you have suspicions, the most important thing to do first is confirm them. You can't take an action so extreme based on feeling alone. Taking a child away from a parent—whether it be the mother or the father—is not the correct course of action unless necessary for the child's safety and well being.

- Look for signs that a mother's behavior is physically or mentally damaging to her child
- Look for signs of child neglect
- Research the mother's past, including criminal history, drug use, domestic violence, etc. Are any of those sectors influencing her present life and actions?
- Determine if the mother has previously had a case open with child protective services
- Consider the home environment; is the child often exposed to situations that are detrimental to his or her upbringing?
- Determine if the mother is abusing substances, such as alcohol or drugs, that could hamper her ability to care properly for her children
- Research the mother's financial situation. Is she capable of adequately supporting the child? Is she spending her income in a way that demonstrates her priorities and the priorities of her child?

- If you're very concerned with the mother's outlook, recommend psychological treatment; if the mother is open to this route, it can help identify the likelihood of her committing abuse or filicide.

Once you've gone through the above steps, if you do see ample evidence that a mother is unfit and putting her child in harm's way, compile evidence (such as pictures, video, audio, correspondence, etc.) that adequately make your case, and then pursue legal means.

When we read through the prior list of actions and consider Casey, it's nearly impossible to find her a fit mother. Red flags fly high left and right: child neglect; drug and alcohol use; financial stability; narcissism. Caylee was constantly exposed to situations that were detrimental to her healthy upbringing. And while at the end of the day Casey must be the one held responsible for Caylee's death—whether by murder or accident—there are plenty of individuals around Casey and Caylee, namely George and Cindy, who should have identified Casey's behaviors as dangerous and removed Caylee from the home.

But hindsight is only helpful if we learn from it. Hillary Clinton once said, "It takes a village to raise a child." I hope you can open your minds and hearts to embrace the idea that it takes a village to *protect* a child. We need to move forward beyond the drama of accused killer "Tot Mom" Casey Anthony. We need to honor all the Caylees of the world by using the mental and emotional energy it took to vigilantly follow the trial and funnel that power to create a safer and healthier environment for children and parents. It may be too late for Caylee, but imagine what we can create as a nation in the protection of our children.

Endnotes

1. David Lohr, "Casey Anthony's Legal Team Shocks Court, Claims Daughter Drowned," *The Huffington Post*, May 24, 2011, http://www.huffingtonpost.com/2011/05/24/casey-anthony-trial-drowning-defense_n_866417.html.

2. Ashley Hayes, "Prosecution, Defense Off Closing Arguments in Casey Anthony Trial," CNN, July 3, 2011, http://articles.cnn.com/2011-07-03/justice/florida.casey.anthony.trial_1_casey-anthony-caylee-jurors?_s=PM:CRIME.

3. Jessica Hopper, "Casey Anthony Trial: Defense Team Claims Caylee Anthony Drowned in Family Pool," ABC News, May 24, 2011, http://abcnews.go.com/US/casey_anthony_trial/casey-anthony-trial-defense-claims-caylee-anthony-drowned/story?id=13674375#.Tsm903OeqWo.

4. R. Leigh Coleman, "Destination Orlando: The Fascination of the Casey Anthony Case," *The Christian Post*, June 28, 2011, http://www.christianpost.com/news/destination-orlando-the-fascination-of-the-casey-anthony-case-51625/.

5. Leslie Horn, "Not Guilty Verdict for Casey Anthony Causes a Surge in Internet Traffic," *PCMag.com*, July 11, 2011, http://www.pcmag.com/article2/0,2817,2388119,00.asp.

6. Chloe Melas, "The Real Reason Casey Anthony was Found Not Guilty," *Holly Baby*, July 5, 2011, http://www.hollybaby.com/2011/07/05/casey-anthony-verdict-not-guilty/.

7. Chloe Melas, "The Real Reason Casey Anthony was Found Not Guilty."

8. "754 Cell Phone Pings in Two Weeks Track Casey – Very Interesting," http://newsgroups.derkeiler.com/Archive/Alt/alt. true-crime/2008-11/msg00235.html.

9. Michael Bouldin, "How Can Police Track Location by a Cell Phone Ping?" *Northern Kentucky Criminal Defense Lawyer*, October 21, 2010, http://nky-criminal-defense-lawyer. com/2010/10/how-can-police-track-location-by-a-cell-phone-ping/.

10. Associated Press, "A Murder a Minute," CBS News, February 11, 2009, http://www.cbsnews.com/stories/2002/10/03/health/main524231.shtml.

11. Patricia Pearson, *When She Was Bad: How And Why Women Get Away With Murder* (Toronto: Random House, 1997).

12. Arlene M. Huysman and Paul J. Goodnick, *The Postpartum Effect: Deadly Depression in Mothers* (New York: Seven Stories Press, 1998).

13. Husyman and Goodnick, *The Postpartum Effect.*

14. Husyman and Goodnick, *The Postpartum Effect.*

15. Jocelyn Noveck, "U.S. has at least 100 incidents per year of mothers killing their children," *Daily Freeman*, April 17, 2011, http://www.dailyfreeman.com/articles/2011/04/17/news/doc4daa3eda5aa4e998808179.txt?viewmode=fullstory.

16. "Parents Who Kill," Missing Madeleine, http://missingmadeleine. forumotion.net/t2334-parents-who-kill-interesting-reading.

17. Steve Pinker, "A Mother's Deadly Secret," *Times of India*, June 9, 2011, http://articles.timesofindia.indiatimes.com/2011-06-09/parenting/28356367_1_car-seats-murders-of-children-age-criminals.

18. Patricia Pearson, *When She Was Bad.*

19. Katherine Ramsland, "Fathers Who Kill," TruTV, http://www.trutv.com/library/crime/criminal_mind/psychology/fathers_who_kill/3.html.

20. Simon Sebag Montefiore, "The Thrill of the Kill," *Psychology Today*, January 1, 1993, http://www.psychologytoday.com/articles/200910/the-thrill-the-kill.

21. Kate Hilpern, "Ending it All," *The Guardian*, September 23, 2008, http://www.guardian.co.uk/society/2008/sep/24/children.mentalhealth.

22. Charles Montaldo, "Women Who Kill Their Children," About.com, http://crime.about.com/od/female_offenders/a/mother_killers.htm.

23. Charles Montaldo, "Women Who Kill Their Children."

24. Patricia Pearson, *When She Was Bad.*

25. Anthony Synnott, *Re-Thinking Men* (Surrey: Ashgate Publishing Limited, 2009).

26. Erin Pizzey, "An Open Letter to Women in the Domestic Violence Movement," http://www.familytx.org/research/articles/PizzyLetter.html.

27. Patricia Pearson, *When She Was Bad.*

28. Ann Japenga, "Ordeal of Postpartum Psychosis: Illness Can Have Tragic Consequences for New Mothers," *Los Angeles Times*, February 1, 1987, http://articles.latimes.com/1987-02-01/news/vw-60_1_postpartum-psychosis.

29. Mikaela Conley, "Public Irate Over Casey Anthony Verdict; Social Media Sites Explode with Opinions," ABC News, July 5, 2011, http://abcnews.go.com/Health/casey-anthony-verdict-outrage-spills-online/story?id=14002257#.TslO3HOeqWo.

30. Dahlia Litwick, "When Parents Kill: Why Fathers Do It. Why Mothers Do It." *Slate*, March 12, 2002, http://www.slate.com/articles/news_and_politics/politics/2002/03/when_parents_kill.html

31. Ashley Hayes, "Casey Anthony Declared Competent; Trial Proceeds," CNN, July 27, 2011, http://articles.cnn.com/2011-06-27/justice/florida.casey.anthony.trial_1_george-and-cindy-anthony-caylee-death-penalty?_s=PM:CRIME.

32. Kenneth J. Ryan, "Casey Anthony Trial: Competency, Insanity, and the Casey Anthony Defense Strategy," *Investigation Discovery*, June 29, 2011, http://blogs.discovery.com/criminal_report/2011/06/casey-anthony-trial-competency-insanity-and-the-casey-anthony-defense-strategy.html.

33. Michael Dowd, "Women and The Abuse Excuse," *Find Law*, http://library.findlaw.com/1999/Nov/1/129404.html.

34. "Casey Anthony, Judgment Day," CBS News, July 5, 2011, http://www.cbsnews.com/stories/2011/07/05/48hours/main20076969.shtml.

35. Jessica Hopper, "Casey Anthony Trial, Her Father Fights Back," June 15, 2011, http://abcnews.go.com/US/casey_anthony_trial/casey-anthonys-father-breaks-daughter-murder-trial/story?id=13840879#.TslSUHOeqWo.

36. Jessica Hopper, "Casey Anthony Trial, Her Father Fights Back."

37. Diane Dimond, "In the Jury's Hands," *The Daily Beast*, July 4, 2011, http://www.thedailybeast.com/articles/2011/07/04/casey-anthony-trial-her-fate-now-it-jury-s-hands.html.

38. Keith Ablow, *Inside the Mind of Casey Anthony: A Psychological Portrait* (2011).

39. "Anthony Lawyers Decry Media Coverage," CNN, July 5, 2011, http://articles.cnn.com/2011-07-05/justice/florida.casey.anthony.lawyers_1_casey-anthony-case-anthony-lawyers-defense-team?_s=PM:CRIME.

40. Meena Hartenstein, "Casey Anthony's Lawyers Blame Media, Salute the Jury for Not Guilty Verdict in Caylee's Murder Trial," *NY Daily News*, July 5, 2011, http://articles.nydailynews.com/2011-07-05/news/29759384_1_casey-anthony-jose-baez-murder-trial.

41. Jessica Hopper, "Casey Anthony Called 'One of the Most Hated Women in America' By Probation," ABC News, August 25, 2011, http://abcnews.go.com/US/casey_anthony_trial/casey-anthony-called-hated-women-america/story?id=14377966#.TsppCnOeqWo.

42. Mary Kate Burke, "Casey Anthony Juror: 'Sick to Our Stomachs' Over Not Guilty Verdict," ABC News, July 6, 2011, http://abcnews.go.com/US/casey_anthony_trial/casey-anthony-juror-jury-sick-stomach-guilty-verdict/story?id=14005609#.TsppbXOeqWo.

43. Mary Kate Burke, "Casey Anthony Juror: 'Sick to Our Stomachs' Over Not Guilty Verdict."

44. Mary Kate Burke, "Casey Anthony Juror: 'Sick to Our Stomachs' Over Not Guilty Verdict."

45. Po Bronson, "Learning to Lie," *NY Magazine*, February 10, 2008, http://nymag.com/news/features/43893/.

46. Po Bronson, "Learning to Lie."

47. Po Bronson, "Learning to Lie."

48. Po Bronson, "Learning to Lie."

49. Po Bronson, "Learning to Lie."

50. Po Bronson, "Learning to Lie."

51. Po Bronson, "Learning to Lie."

52. Mayo Clinic, "Anti Social Personality Disorder," http://www.mayoclinic.com/health/antisocial-personality-disorder/DS00829.

53. Scott Stump, "Former Fiance: Anthony Family a 'Carnival of Dysfunctionality," MSNBC, July 6, 2011, http://today.msnbc.msn.com/id/43652425/ns/today-today_people/t/former-fiance-anthony-family-carnival-dysfunctionality/#.TspdE3OeqWo

54. Diane Dimond, "Casey's Roommate Tells All," *The Daily Beast*, June 22, 2011, http://www.thedailybeast.com/articles/2011/06/22/casey-s-rommate-tells-all.html.

55. Tommy Garrett, "Shocking Allegations in Casey Anthony Case," *Canyon News*, July 3, 2011, http://www.canyon-news.com/artman2/publish/National_News_1182/Shocking_Allegations_In_Casey_Anthony_Case_Exclusive.php.

56. Jennifer L. Tanner, "Was Casey Anthony an 'Adult?' I Wish Someone Would Have Asked" *Psychology Today*, July 6, 2011, http://www.psychologytoday.com/blog/becoming-adult/201107/was-casey-anthony-adult-i-wish-someone-would-have-asked.

57. Jennifer L. Tanner, "Was Casey Anthony an 'Adult?' I Wish Someone Would Have Asked."

58. Jennifer L. Tanner, "Was Casey Anthony an 'Adult?' I Wish Someone Would Have Asked."

59. Evelyn Leite, "Which Comes First Passive Men or Controlling Women," *Self Growth*, http://www.selfgrowth.com/articles/which_comes_first_passive_men_or_controlling_women.

60. "Cindy Anthony's Brother Speaks," Casey Anthony Trial Today in Review, http://caseyanthonytrialtodayinreview.blogspot.com/2011/07/cindy-anthonys-brother-speaks-trascript.html.

61. Jacqui Goddard, "Casey Anthony's Father Denies Having an Affair with Volunteer Who Searched for Caylee's Body," *Mail Online*, June 28, 2011, http://www.dailymail.co.uk/news/article-2009169/Casey-Anthony-murder-trial-Father-George-denies-affair-Crystal-Holloway.html.

62. Dr. Lillian Glass, "Jury Foreman on Casey Anthony Case Said George Anthony's Body Language Turned Everyone Off," Dr. Lillian Glass Body Language, July 12, 2011, http://drlillianglassbodylanguageblog.wordpress.com/2011/07/12/jury-foreman-on-casey-anthony-case-said-george-anthonys-body-language-turned-everyone-off/

63. David Lohr, "Casey Anthony's Father, George Anthony, Tells Dr. Phil He Blames Her for Caylee's Death," *Huffington Post*, September 14, 2011, http://www.huffingtonpost.com/mobileweb/1969/12/31/_n_963232.html.

64. Scott Stump, "Dr. Phil: Cindy Anthony has 'denial of highest order,'" *Today*, September 14, 2011, http://today.msnbc.msn.com/id/44517028/ns/today-today_people/t/dr-phil-cindy-anthony-has-denial-highest-order/#.TspkIXOeqWo.

65. Scott Stump, "Dr. Phil: Cindy Anthony has 'denial of highest order.'"

66. Jessica Hopper, "Casey Anthony Overdosed Caylee, George Anthony Charges," ABC News, September 14, 2011, http://abcnews.go.com/US/casey-anthony-drugged-caylee-george-anthony-charges/story?id=14518857#.TsplHXOeqWo.

67. David Lohr, "Casey Anthony's Father, George Anthony, Tells Dr. Phil He Blames Her for Caylee's Death."

68. "Cindy and George Anthony: The Most Hated Grandparents in America?" http://latimesblogs.latimes.com/nationnow/2011/09/cindy-and-george-anthony-the-most-hated-grandparents-in-america.html.

69. Carl Pickhardt, "Surviving (Your Child's) Adolescence," *Psychology Today*, October 25, 2010, http://www.psychologytoday.com/blog/surviving-your-childs-adolescence/201010/adolescence-parental-disappointment-and-parental-guilt.

70. Jennifer Tanner, "Casey Anthony is Normal, That's the Problem," *Psychology Today*, June 17, 2011, http://www.psychologytoday.com/blog/becoming-adult/201106/casey-anthony-is-normal-thats-the-problem.

71. Scott Stump, "Former Fiance: Anthony Family a 'Carnival of Dysfunctionality."

72. Timothy Roche, "Andrea Yates: More to the Story," *Time Magazine*, March 18, 2002, http://www.time.com/time/nation/article/0,8599,218445,00.html.

73. "Andrea Yates Case: Yates Found Not Guilty by Reason of Insanity," CNN, December 11, 2007, http://articles.cnn.com/2007-12-11/us/court.archive.yates8_1_russell-rusty-yates-kaylynn-williford-joe-owmby?_s=PM:US.

74. Jocelyn Noveck, "U.S. has at least 100 incidents per year of mothers killing their children," Daily Freeman, April 17, 2011, http://www.dailyfreeman.com/articles/2011/04/17/news/doc4daa3eda5aa4e998808179.txt

75. Associated Press, "Moms Killing Children Not Nearly as Rare as We Think," *The Boston Herald*, April 16, 2011, http://www.bostonherald.com/news/national/general/view.bg?articleid=1331175.

76. "Build on Your Strengths – Mental Health Awareness Month" University of Toronto, http://life.utoronto.ca/Stories_Etc/Build_on_your_Strengths_-_Mental_Health_Awareness_Month.htm.

77. "Epidemiology of Mental Illness" *Mental Health: A Report of the Surgeon General*, http://www.surgeongeneral.gov/library/mentalhealth/chapter2/sec2_1.html.

78. Juan Salinas, http://homepage.psy.utexas.edu/homepage/class/Psy301/Salinas/06PsychologicalDisorders.htm.

79. Jocelyn Noveck, "Mothers Who Kill Children," *Huffington Post*, April 16, 2011, http://www.huffingtonpost.com/2011/04/16/mother-kill-children-society-_n_850094.html

80. Jocelyn Noveck, "U.S. has at least 100 incidents per year of mothers killing their children."

81. Marisol Bello, "Casey Anthony Faces Many Challenges Once Freed," *USA Today*, July 6, 2011, http://www.usatoday.com/news/nation/2011-07-06-casey-anthony-what-next_n.htm.

82. Dr. Drew, "Casey Anthony: After the Verdict Transcript," CNN, July 11, 2011, http://transcripts.cnn.com/TRANSCRIPTS/1107/11/ddhln.01.html.

83. Steven Pinker, "A Mother's Deadly Secret," *The Times of India*, June 9, 2011, http://articles.timesofindia.indiatimes.com/2011-06-09/parenting/28356367_1_car-seats-murders-of-children-age-criminals.

84. Carla Rivera, "Child Abuse in U.S. at Crisis Level, Panel Says," *Los Angeles Times*, April 26, 1995, http://articles.latimes.com/1995-04-26/news/mn-59137_1_child-abuse-authority.

85. Patricia Pearson, *When She Was Bad*.

86. Patricia Pearson, *When She Was Bad*.

87. Robert Oliphant and Nancy Ver Steegh, *Family Law: Examples and Explanations* (New York: Aspen Publishers, 2007).

88. Richard A. Lippa, *Gender, Nature, Nurture* (New Jersey: 2002).

Acknowledgements

To *Joel Sachs*, who I am grateful to more than any words can express. Thank you for your total and absolute belief in me. Thanks for your unwavering support of my dream to help others live *Excuse Free™*. Mashed potatoes and scotch make a fine team.

I thank my *family* for the variety of ways each of you have chosen to support my vision writing this book. To my nephew, Shane, and niece, Olivia: all dreams are possible if you are willing to do the work. I am proud of you both.

Thank you to *Megan Byrd*, my amazing editor who turned grapes into wine. Your grace, intelligence, and talent made the process of writing joyful.

To *David Dunham* and Dunham Books, thank you for giving me the opportunity to share the truth with the public, no matter how controversial, of women and mothers accused of murdering in cold blood.

Thank you to *all of the producers* of the *Nancy Grace Show* for all of your hard work, as well as (CNN/HLN) *CNN Headline News* for opening the door and keeping it open. A special thanks to producer *Greg Overzat,* and executive producer *Dean Sicoli,* who trusted me and my professional opinion throughout the Casey Anthony trial.

To *Nancy Grace*, thank you for countless opportunities you've given me. Without question, your generosity, keen observation, and kindness have been and continue to be life changing. Your ability to work through and overcome adversity, along with your refusal to make excuses related to your extraordinarily painful loss, is an inspiration to women everywhere. You have used your tragedy to find a life of meaning serving others and advocating for children. Your character is, without question, honorable—matched only by your boundless integrity and the size of your heart.

Mark Geragos, you are a force to be reckoned with. My respect for you and gratitude to you is boundless. I will forever remember your thoughtfulness and kindheartedness. Thank you for shedding light on the legal and psychological process of the jury system. Without this understanding, the American people are left with nothing more than anger and frustration. But, with information there can one day be change.

To my longtime friend and colleague, *Eugene Matthews, aka* *"Chip."* Your support of this book and input has been nothing short of invaluable. As a lawyer and consultant to high-level executives, companies, and corporations, you not only keep your word, you deliver and get results. You are a rarity in general and even more so in tough economic times.

To my publicist, Guttman Associates Vice President, *Rona Menashe*, and junior associate Lyndsi Turner, thank you for your honesty, integrity, and hard work.

To *Karen Wulfson*, thank you for your unwavering belief in me. You are an outstanding psychotherapist and human being.

To my *friends* who gave their unconditional support and made this process celebratory: Kathy Tiberi, Laura Hertz, and my Lago family!

And finally, to little *Moet* who sat by me and in my lap watching mama type away, giving lots of kisses and tail wags.

About the Author

Dr. Leslie Seppinni is a distinguished Doctor of Clinical Psychology and a Licensed Marriage Family Therapist with 18 years experience specializing in Cognitive Behavioral therapy. A prominent public speaker on topics ranging from self-empowerment to relationships and managing stress, Dr. Leslie shares her Excuse Free™ philosophy with people seeking to create positive change in their lives.

Dr. Seppinni was a regular contributor on Nancy Grace's CNN show during the Casey Anthony trial and appears regularly, providing unique insight to the media on a wide spectrum of psychological, lifestyle and breaking news topics. She often appears on shows such as *Good Morning America, CBS Evening News with Katie Couric,* wallstreetjournal.com, CNN's *Nancy Grace Show,* Fox News.com, CNBC's *The Call,* and numerous outlets throughout the country. In addition, she is regularly quoted in popular publications, including *The New York Times,* the *Associated Press, Forbes,* BusinessWeek. com, *USA Weekend,* the *Washington Post, Newsweek, Bariatrics Today, Self, More, First, InTouch,* and *Women's Health.*

Mentoring individuals is one of Dr. Leslie's many charitable services, including the recent donation of six "Excuse Free Living" life coaching sessions to five people around the country. Her last mentoree graduated from Harvard in December 2009. She also served for several years as a committee member for UCLA Scholarships for Disadvantaged Students. Ice Skating in Harlem, Bottomless Closet, Jordan Downs High School, and The Children's Defense Fund New Orleans are among other recipients of her philanthropy.

She holds a Doctorate in Clinical Psychology from Ryokan College, a Master 's in Counseling Psychology from the University of Southern California (USC) and a Bachelor's in Sociology from UCLA.